Listen, Mother of God!

D1111333

Reflections on the Litany of Loreto

Msgr. Charles Dollen

Our Sunday Visitor Publishing Division
Our Sunday Visitor, Inc.
Huntington, Indiana 46750

International Standard Book Number:
0-87973-427-2
Library of Congress Catalog Card Number:
89-60266

Cover design by Rebecca J. O'Brien

Published, printed, and bound in the U.S.A. by
Our Sunday Visitor Publishing Division
Our Sunday Visitor, Inc.
200 Noll Plaza
Huntington, IN 46750

427

Dedicated to

James J. Daley
1934-1987

Acknowledgments

Scripture quotes have been taken from The St. Joseph Edition of the *New American Bible* and *The Holy Bible*, Douay Version. Also consulted were *The New Jerusalem Bible* and *The New Testment* translated by Msgr. Ronald Knox.

Most of the other quotations were taken from my previously published anthologies and works:
The Book of Catholic Wisdom. Our Sunday Visitor.
The Catholic Tradition. Consortium.
Civil Rights: A Source Book. St. Paul Editions.
Jesus, Lord! St. Paul Editions.
Marmion: Fire of Love. Herder.
My Rosary: Its Power and Mystery. Alba House.
Prayerbook of the Saints. Our Sunday Visitor.
Prayers for the Third Age. Our Sunday Visitor
Prophecies Fulfilled. Our Sunday Visitor
A Voice Said Ave! St. Paul Editions.

The volume most frequently used was:
Blunt, Hugh F., *Listen, Mother of God*. Catholic Literary Guild. 1940.

Other works consulted or quoted:
Alberione, James, *Mary, Hope of the World* in *Life of the Madonna in Art*. St. Paul Editions.
Alphonsus Liguori, St., *The Glories of Mary*. Redemptorist Fathers.
Ball, Ann, *A Litany of Mary*. Our Sunday Visitor.
Book of Mary, USCC Secretariate, Bishop's Committee on the Liturgy.
Britt, Matthew, *Hymns of the Breviary and Missal*. Burns, Oates, Washburn.
Buddy, Charles Francis, *For Them Also*. University of San Diego Press.

Foy, Felician, *1988 Catholic Almanac*. Our Sunday Visitor.

Heffernan, Virginia Mary, *Outlines of the 16 Documents of Vatican II*. America Press.

Lynch, John W., *A Woman Wrapped in Silence*. Macmillan.

Marmion, Columba, *Christ in His Mysteries*. Herder. *Christ the Life of the Soul*. Herder.

McKenzie, John, *Dictionary of the Bible*. Bruce.

Moran, Patrick, *Day by Day with Mary*. Our Sunday Visitor. *Day by Day with the Saints*. Our Sunday Visitor. *The New Catholic Encyclopedia*.

O'Carroll, Michael, *Theotokos*. Glazier.

O'Connell, Daniel M., *Favorite Newman Sermons*. America Press.

Power, Albert, *Our Lady's Titles*. Pustet.

Sherley-Price, Leo, *Queen of Peace*. Pax House.

Sixteen Documents of Vatican II. St. Paul Editions.

Walsh, John J., *Thirteenth: The Greatest of Centuries*. Catholic Summer School Press

The following pamphlets were helpful:
Gorman, Paul, *Life with Joseph*. Leaflet Missal Co.

Neubert, E., *My Ideal: Jesus Son of Mary*. Maryhurst Press.

Resch, Peter A., *Our Mother: A Simple Mariology*. St. Meinrad/Grail.

Schultzenberg, Mark, *The Jewel of God*. Leaflet Missal Co.

The quotations from the Papal Encyclicals were taken from my anthologies, or from the *New Catholic Encyclopedia,* except for the following:
John Paul II, *Mother of the Redeemer*. St. Paul Editions.

Contents

1

The Litany of Loreto

In 1940 Father Hugh F. Blunt wrote a book on the Litany of Loreto, or as it is more popularly known, the Litany of Our Lady, which to this day has a place of favor in many Catholic libraries. With loving devotion from his rich Irish tradition, he investigated each title in the Litany with theological skill.

A litany is a form of prayer in which the leader prays a series of praises and petitions and the people reply with a set refrain. The most familiar to us are the *Kyrie Eleison* and the *Agnus Dei* of the Mass. Another form is the Solemn Prayers of the Good Friday Liturgy.

The most beautiful example in the Bible is Psalm 136, in which the refrain, repeated over and over again is "His mercy endures forever." It is not typical of Jewish prayers, however, since all Jewish men were supposed to know how to read, and the Old Testament prayers could be shared by the whole synagogue or temple worshipers.

The oldest litany in continuous use by Christians is the Litany of the Saints. In a form we would be familiar with, it goes back at least to the eighth century, but that is a reflection of much more ancient versions and petitions. It is used in ordinations and at other solemn occasions.

Our Lady's Litany, in its present form, goes back to the sixteenth century, and it was built on a series of praises in regular use at the Shrine of Loreto in the twelfth century. This present form was made popular by St. Peter Canisius, S.J. in 1558. There is an Irish version going back at least to the eighth century.

The Shrine of Loreto, one of the most famous places of Marian pilgrimages since the thirteenth century, contains what is purported to be the Holy House of

Nazareth, where the Holy Family lived during Our Lord's "hidden years." It bears up remarkably well under critical investigations, many of which have been conducted over the centuries.

According to some, angels transported the home to Loreto, an Italian town on the Adriatic Sea. Others feel it was English crusaders or pilgrims who brought the relic. It hinges on whether it was "angeli" or "Angli" who were responsible.

Litanies were so popular during the time of the Counter-Reformation, that popes stepped in to regulate their use. For many centuries, the only litanies approved for public use were the Litany of the Saints and the Litany of Loreto. Now several others can be found in various prayer books, such as the Litany of the Sacred Heart and the Litany of St. Joseph.

In recent years, dissatisfaction has been voiced about the translations of some of the titles, especially those which refer to particular Marian praises.

The International Committee on English in the Liturgy, Inc. (ICEL) has just issued a new and approved translation which is referred to in this book in the chapter headings.

In the past century only five titles have been added to the Litany, the most recent title being added by Pope Pius XII on the occasion of the definition of the Assumption of the Blessed Mother on November 1, 1950.

The Litany has four main series of praises. After a suitable introduction, the first series salutes Mary as Mother, the second series as Virgin, the third by particular titles and the fourth as Queen.

Many of the great saints nourished their spiritual lives on this Litany, such as St. Charles Borromeo, St. Alphonsus Liguori, St. Francis de Sales and St. Ignatius Loyola.

St. Augustine points out that whatever we may say in praise of Mary is very little in comparison with what she deserves. The insistent refrain, begging for Mary's intercession, is like the lover's plea to be heard. It is like the child who tags after the mother until she cannot fail to heed the voice. It is a cry of faith addressed to the Mother of God for her maternal help in our lives.

Through it runs the theme — Listen, Mother of God!

Litany of Loreto

Lord, have mercy.
Christ, have mercy.
Lord, have mercy.
Christ, hear us.
Christ, graciously hear us.
God, the Father of heaven:
Have mercy on us.
God, the Son, redeemer of the world:
Have mercy on us.
God, the Holy Spirit:
Have mercy on us.
Holy Trinity, one God:
Have mercy on us.
Holy Mary:
pray for us.
Holy Mother of God:
Holy Virgin of Virgins:
Mother of Christ:
Mother of Divine Grace:
Mother Most Pure:
Mother Most Chaste:
Mother Inviolate:
Mother Undefiled:
Mother Most Lovable:
  (Mother Most Amiable)
  (Dearest of Mothers)
Mother Most Admirable:
  (Model of Motherhood)
  (Mother Most Wonderful)
Mother of Good Counsel:
Mother of Our Creator:
Mother of Our Savior:
  (Mother of Our Redeemer)
Mother of the Church:
Virgin Most Prudent:
  (Virgin Most Wise)
Virgin Most Venerable:

(Virgin Rightly Praised
Virgin Most Renowned:
 (Virgin Rightly Renowned)
Virgin Most Powerful:
Virgin Most Merciful:
 (Virgin Gentle in Mercy)
Virgin Most Faithful:
 (Faithful Virgin)
Mirror of Justice:
Seat of Wisdom:
 (Throne of Wisdom)
Cause of Our Joy:
Spiritual Vessel:
 (Shrine of the Soul)
Vessel of Honor:
 (Glory of Israel)
Singular Vessel of Devotion:
 (Vessel of Selfless Devotion)
Mystical Rose:
Tower of David:
Tower of Ivory:
House of Gold:
Ark of the Covenant:
Gate of Heaven:
Morning Star:
Health of the Sick:
Refuse of Sinners:
Comforter of the Afflicted:
Help of Christians:
Queen of Angels:
Queen of Patriarchs and Queen of Prophets:
Queen of Apostles and Martyrs:
Queen of Confessors and Virgins:
Queen of All Saints:
Queen Conceived Without Original Sin:
Queen Assumed Into Heaven:
Queen of the Rosary:
Queen of Peace:

2
Holy Mary

The holy name of Mary has always puzzled the scholars. It comes from the ancient Hebrew form, *Miryam*, but they can't even agree on what that name means.

Some would translate it as "exalted," and they see it as a reference to her dignity as Mother of God. Others claim that it means "bitter," and so refer it to her suffering along with Christ during His passion and death.

When it came to translating the name into Latin, *Maria*, the name immediately brought up the image of the sea from the word *mar*, meaning the sea. Since the image of the Church as the barque of Peter on the sea of the world was very popular, the idea of Mary as the star of the sea helping to guide that ship was often used. St. Bernard's passage in his second *Missus Est* homily is a classic in this interpretation:

"And the virgin's name was Mary. Let us say a few things about that name which can be interpreted to mean 'Star of the Sea.' An apt designation for the virgin Mother.

"She is most beautifully likened to a star, for a star pours forth its light without losing anything of its nature. She gave us her Son without losing anything of her virginity. The glowing rays of a star take nothing from its beauty. Neither has the Son taken anything away from his Mother's integrity.

"She is that noble star of Jacob, illuminating the whole world, penetrating from the highest heavens to the lowest depths of hell. The warmth of her brilliance shines in the minds of men, encouraging virtue, extinguishing vice. She is that glorious star lighting the way across the vast ocean of life, glowing with merits, guiding by example.

"When you find yourself tossed by the raging waters on this great sea of life, far from land, keep your eyes fixed on this star to avoid disaster. When the winds of temptation or the rocks of tribulation threaten, look up to the star, call upon Mary!

"When the waves of pride or ambition sweep over you, when the tide of detraction or jealousy runs against you, look up to the star, call upon Mary! When the shipwreck of avarice, anger or lust seems imminent, call upon Mary!

"If the horror of sin overwhelms you and the voice of conscience terrifies you, if the fear of judgment, the abyss of sadness and the depths of despair clutch at your heart, think of Mary! In dangers, difficulties and doubts, think about Mary, call upon Mary!"

We address Mary as "holy" with great theological accuracy. Holiness involves union with God through the gift of the sanctifying grace won for us by Christ. Through this gift, freely given by God, the human will is united with the will of God, evidenced by the practice of virtue and the avoidance of sin.

She appears at the beginning of the Christian dispensation with the salutation from the Archangel Gabriel, "Hail, full of grace." Without quibbling over the various ways that greeting might be translated, Catholic devotion has always given it this full and literal meaning. Mary's soul was filled with grace from its very beginning as a fit and suitable preparation for her vocation as Mother of God. She was the First Christian in every sense of the term.

Her response to the angelic situation was, "Be it done to me according to your word." Her submission to the will of God was total and complete. It sets the pace for her entire life in the Christian economy of salvation. Every treasured glimpse we have of her in the New Testament confirms this union with God's will.

Perhaps everyone's favorite example of this is at the

Marriage Feast at Cana. Her loving heart goes out to the embarrassed bride and groom when the wine fails. She turns to Jesus for a miracle without any hesitation. How well she knew her Jesus! Had there, perhaps, been many miracles at her intercession during the Hidden Life?

Catholic devotion has always delighted in singing the praises of this woman. With her *fiat*, she healed the wound dealt to human nature by Eve. In an applied sense, she is the woman clothed with the Sun in Revelations, so that, as some have remarked, the Bible begins and ends with Mary.

St. Jerome, the eminent scripture scholar, says, "What is there to name Mary but sanctification!" Well does the modern poet call her, "Our tainted nature's solitary boast."

Dorothy Day, a practical lady of common-sense spirituality, has this to offer: "So I am trying to learn to recall my soul like the straying creature it is as it wanders off over and over again during the day, and lift my heart to the Blessed Mother and the saints, since my occupations are the lowly and humble ones, as were theirs."

The holiness of Mary attracts us to her Son like a magnet.

3

Holy Mother of God

Real devotion to Mary always leads to a greater appreciation and understanding of the Incarnation, a greater love of her Son Jesus, the God-man. The fact of the divine maternity, that Mary is the Mother of God, is the basic tenet underlying all Mariology.

To us, the gospel facts seem obvious and beyond dispute. Mary is really the Mother of Jesus and Jesus is truly the Son of God. Therefore, Mary is the Mother of God. The divine maternity is a gospel fact.

However, early heretics, trying to deny the divinity of Christ, or His humanity, had to attack the position of the Virgin Mother. St. Ignatius of Antioch, St. Justin Martyr and St. Irenaeus were among the early Church Fathers who came to her defense.

Irenaeus says boldly, "God was brought forth by Mary."

In the fifth century, when a particularly virulent heresy tried to deny the divinity of Christ, the Church at the Council of Ephesus in A.D. 431 stated definitively that God is truly *Emmanuel*, "and therefore that the Holy Virgin is the Mother of God."

The Council used the term *Theotokos*, God-bearer. Therefore, in the strictest sense, in the literal sense, without figure of speech, hair-splitting or subterfuge, Mary is the Mother of God.

Origin was the first writer known to have used this term, *Theotokos*, but when Nestorious tried to change it to Christ-bearer, to deny Christ's divinity, St. Athanasius took him to task in no uncertain terms.

The theologians like to examine this truth further, as they do all the truths and mysteries of religion. Jesus Christ is one person, and that person is the second Person of the Blessed Trinity. That person is

God; He has the divine nature. This He received from His Father, in eternity, the only-begotten Son of God.

In the fullness of time, as St. Paul states, He entered into human history by taking a human nature from the Blessed Virgin Mary. This is a mother-son relationship.

When a mother leans out the window and calls her son, she does not say, "Body that I bore," or "Human nature that I conceived," she calls her son. And so it was with Mary. When she called Jesus, she called her son.

Therefore, every action Jesus performed can be attributed to the person in whichever nature they were performed. An earlier author in this century wrote a book on the Passion, Death and Resurrection of Christ. He titled the book *God Died at Three O'Clock!*

One of the earliest Marian prayers, still a favorite among many people, begins, "We fly to your patronage, O holy Mother of God."

St. Thomas Aquinas, when speaking of this great title of Mary says, "There cannot be anything better." It is the most sublime title that could ever be given to a mere creature. Cardinal Newman says that so vital is the fact of the Divine Maternity that the existence or ruin of a church depends on it.

Benedictine Abbot Columba Marmion, writing early in this century, reminds us that Christ could have come into the world in any number of ways, but instead He chose to be born of Mary. "That is a unique privilege that Mary shares with none."

We could easily become lost in the wonder of this sublime relationship. We cannot praise God enough for the wonders His grace has confirmed in Mary. But we have a real stake in this mystery.

Mary is our Mother, too. The saints like to meditate on the words of Christ on the Cross — to Mary, "Behold your son!" and to John, "Behold your mother!" — and see in them a sharing of Mary's maternal role with all mankind, and certainly with all Christians. Theologically, the relationship is even more real. Christ is the Head of His Church, the Mystical Body. Mary, who is the Mother of the Head of the Church, is also, therefore, the Mother of the members of that Church.

Throughout the first part of the Litany, the refrain "Mother . . . mother . . . mother," is repeated over and over again. We make our own the sentiment of St. Stanislaus Kostka, who, when asked how much he loved the Blessed Virgin, replied, "What else I can say? She is my Mother."

4

Holy Virgin of Virgins

In 1962, while I was serving as a reserve chaplain in the U.S. Navy, my two closest friends were two very fine Lutheran chaplains who guided me through those first trying months.

Our conversations frequently turned to theological points, long before ecumenism was a very popular movement. One of them said one day, "You know I could easily become a Roman Catholic if you didn't worship the Virgin Mary."

My answer was not very ecumenical, I'm afraid, and I went home fuming. Roman Catholics do not worship the Mother of God. Honor, veneration, love and the like, but worship is reserved to God alone — we all know that.

To see how the Church responds to Mary, I started checking the Fathers and Doctors of the Church. In fact, my first book, entitled *A Voice Said Ave!*, grew out of that research, (Boston, St. Paul Editions, 1963).

Two striking facts emerged from that research. The Fathers, Doctors, saints, scripture scholars and theologians were truly unanimous in their belief in the ever-sinlessness and the ever-virginity of the Blessed Mother. She was recognized as completely without sin and as a perpetual virgin.

Did someone deny Christ had a body? They pointed to the Nativity, to the Virgin Mother. Did someone deny that Christ was always the Son of God? They proclaimed Mary as Mother of God. Over and over, the theology of the Incarnation was defended by the divine maternity of the ever-virgin, ever-sinless Mary.

It was a remarkable testimony to what the Church believed and what it proclaimed.

St. Jerome, commenting on Ezekiel, says, "The

Blessed Virgin Mary is that beautiful closed gate. She was a virgin before childbirth and she remained a virgin after childbirth. To the Virgin an angel said, 'The Holy Spirit shall come over you and the power of the most high God shall overshadow you; the Holy One to be born of you will be called the Son of God.' She remained a virgin after He was born. Forever, Mary is a virgin.

"Some have falsely claimed that the 'brethren of the Lord' mentioned in Scripture are children born to Mary from Joseph. This is definitely wrong to say about the ever-Virgin Mary, who is the closed gate that will not be opened."

And in the book against Jovinian he remarks, "Christ was a virgin and his Mother was ever-virgin."

St. Augustine adds his testimony, "A virgin conceiving, a virgin bearing a child, a virgin pregnant, a virgin fruitful, a virgin forever! Why should you marvel at this? For God had so to be born as He condescended to become a man."

Three points, then are contained in this dogma: the virginal conception of Jesus by Mary without any human father; the virginal birth of the child from the womb of His mother without any injury to her bodily integrity; and Mary's observance of virginity afterward throughout her earthly life.

For many of the Fathers of the Church, this virgin birth and its miraculous character has less to do with the privileges of Mary than as a glory to Christ and the beginning of the rebirth of the human race.

For St. Matthew, the virginity of Mary had been proclaimed by the Prophet Isaiah, " 'Behold, the virgin shall be with child and bear a son and they shall name him Emmanuel,' which means 'God is with us' " (Is 7:14; Mt 1:23). Here we have an inspired writer interpreting an inspired text. This was the meaning accepted by the early theologians and scripture scholars. Its beauty is breathtaking! Did Mary have a vow of virginity? That is a conclusion of many of the saints, not the least of whom is St. Thomas Aquinas. He quotes St. Augustine with approval when that holy bishop writes: "Mary replied to the angel at the Annunciation, 'How shall this be brought about since I do not have relations with men?' What she was saying in effect was that she had already vowed her virginity."

Vows were well known among the Jews and, indeed, we know that St. Paul took a vow at one time. When Mary replied to Gabriel, "I do not know man," the original Greek uses a verb form that emphasizes the permanence of the action. What form that permanence had in Mary's determination may have been a vow both in fact and in effect.

It is impossible to guess how much effect this doctrine of the perpetual virginity of Mary has had on the spiritual life of the Church. Through the Christian centuries, many young men and women have vowed themselves to God in virginity, chastity and celibacy, inspired by their love for the Blessed Virgin.

At times, when the world has said that sex cannot be controlled, many young people have lived chaste lives for love of God, in imitation of Christ, with an added devotion to Mary. Marital fidelity has also been inspired by her courageous determination.

It is even a tribute to the God-given beauty of human sexuality that chastity has so much spiritual value. After all, if human sexuality were not a splendid thing, giving up the use of it as a sacrifice would hardly be pleasing to God.

Cardinal Newman adds, "To have a virgin soul is to love nothing on earth in comparison of God, or except for his sake. That soul is virginal which is ever looking for its Beloved, who is in heaven, and which sees him in whatever is lovely upon earth, loving earthly friends very dearly, but in their proper place, as his gifts and representatives, and loving Jesus alone with sovereign affection, and bearing to lose all to keep him."

5
Mother of Christ

When we salute Mary as "Mother of God," we can offer no higher praise. All her other titles are summed up in that title, all her claims upon us.

The human mind, however, is so limited in the face of the infinite God that we need to expand whatever knowledge we have, as much as we can. Abbot Columba Marmion, O.S.B. remarks that, "we can only lisp when we speak of God."

So, in praising the Blessed Mother of God, we need to look at all the aspects of Mariology that flow from her principle title. That she is the Mother of the God-man, the Mother of the Word Incarnate, focuses our attention on her relationship to her Son as the Divine One.

"Mother of Christ" helps us emphasize the fact of the humanity of the Son of God. The name given Him, Jesus, points out the fact that He is the Savior of the world; the title Christ tells us that He is the anointed one, the Messiah, the fulfillment of a long line of prophecy, the hope of all the ages since Adam and Eve.

St. Gregory of Nyssa reminds us that "Paul teaches us the power of Christ's name when he calls him the power and wisdom of God, our peace, the unapproachable light where God dwells, our expiation and redemption, our great High Priest . . . ."

He goes on to speak of Him as "the mighty God, the Head of his body, the Church, the firstborn of the new creation, the Mediator between God and man, the only-begotten crowned with glory and honor."

St. Bernard cries out in his hymn, *Jesu Dulcis Memoria*: "O hope of every contrite heart, O joy of all the meek, / To those who fall how kind you are, / How good to those who seek."

And he adds elsewhere, "The name of Jesus is honey in the mouth, music to the ear, a cry of gladness in the heart!"

This Jesus was the Savior of the world from the first instant of His creation in the womb of the Blessed Mother. St. Gregory puts it this way, "At the moment the angel announced it, in the instant when the Holy Spirit overshadowed her, in that very moment the Word entered her womb. At that very instant the Word became flesh."

Commenting on this, St. Thomas Aquinas rephrases it, "The actual moment in which he took flesh, the moment in which the body was animated, that was instantaneous. . . In the very instant in which the material came to the place of generation, the body of Christ was perfectly formed and assumed by him."

The title Christ shows what His life's work was to be. He came into the world to do His Father's will, and that will was our salvation. Jesus, Savior, was anointed, to be our holy Redeemer.

All the messianic prophecies of the Old Testament pointed the way to Him. All the great figures of salvation history led the way to Him. In the Garden of Eden, the savior was promised in a passage the Fathers of the Church heralded as the Protevangelium (Gen 3:15).

Abraham, Isaac, Jacob, Moses, the Judges, David and Solomon were, at times, figures of the saving nature of Christ's mission. The early Christian Church loved the prophets, especially Isaiah, because he seemed to foretell so many details of Christ's life. St. Matthew's Gospel makes heavy use of the messianic prophecies.

St. Bernard wrote many things about the Annunciation, but perhaps his most dramatic scene is his picture of the moment between the time when Gabriel announced his good news and Our Lady responded.

Bernard has Adam and Eve, the patriarchs and prophets, the Kings and priests, and, indeed, all the host of the heavenly court collectively holding their breath, then begging her to acquiesce. At her *fiat*, all of Heaven breaks into jubilant praise of God for the workings of His grace.

Mary had free will, so theoretically it was possible that she could have said, "No." If she had refused, how long would we have waited for the coming of Christ? Would it have meant many more centuries of longing for the savior? Would we still be waiting?

But in reality, of course, Mary's will was so perfectly in accord with the will of God that there was simply no question of her agreement. As we know from the first two chapters of St. Luke's Gospel, Mary's spirituality had been formed by the Old Testament, and the coming of the Messiah was the goal she shared with her beloved countrymen.

It was the common teaching of the rabbis of her day, and the general expectation of the "people of the land" with whom she identified, that Daniel's prophecy of the weeks (of years) for the coming of the Messiah were at hand.

This explains why there were so many rebellions against Rome, led by false messiahs. That was because, except for the more holy expectations of the simpler folk, the members of an oppressed nation emphasized the victorious nature of the Christ's advent and looked for a political savior.

That Christ would restore the rule to Israel and rejuvenate the House of David in the material realm was not to be. His kingdom was not of this world, and His rule was to be, quite simply and literally, eternal. He was, indeed, the Liberator, but in the much more important sphere of the spiritual.

Mary's appreciation of this fact seems evident from her *Magnificat*, and from the interchange with Elizabeth at the Visitation and with Simeon at the Presentation. Mary, the Mother of Christ, was with Him throughout His earthly life. She is unmistakably present throughout the Gospels. She bursts on the scene, of course, at the Annunciation, which Bishop John Lancaster Spalding commemorates so beautifully with his verse on the Angelus bells:

At dawn the joyful choir of bells
In consecrated citadels,
Flings to the sweet and drowsy air
A brief, melodious call to prayer;
For Mary, Virgin meek and lowly
Conceived of the Spirit Holy,
As the Lord's angel did declare.

6
Mother of Divine Grace

Jesus is the fountainhead and source of all grace. He is Divine Grace itself, and every grace that we human beings receive comes from Him alone. He alone merited this complete treasury of grace by His Paschal sacrifice and triumph.

Since Mary is His Mother, by her connection with Him, she is the Mother of Divine Grace. All the singular graces she received came from her Son. Far from taking any glory away from Him, the graces He shares with her are an additional triumph of Christ.

The Church loves to sing of this triumph of the Grace of God in the soul of the Blessed Mother. It applies to her the words from the Book of Proverbs: "Many daughters have gathered riches, but you have surpassed them all." And again: "Grace is poured forth from your lips, therefore God has blessed you for ever and ever."

St. Thomas Aquinas tells us that "the fact that she was the Mother of God gave her a special office, and so she must have special holiness." Other theologians speak of her "supremacy of holiness," or that she is "an abyss of grace."

That holiness grew day by day, moment by moment. She who was full of grace at the time of the Annunciation became ever more Christ-like as her years with Him passed. The combined graces of all the members of the heavenly court do not equal what God has caused in her soul.

Often when we address the Blessed Mother, we use the language of love, which allows for a little exaggeration. How many love songs speak of climbing the highest mountains or swimming the deepest rivers to prove a human love. But when we address Mary as the

Mother of Divine Grace, we are speaking theological truths. There is no need for pious exaggeration.

Not only is she herself filled with grace, God has willed to channel His graces to us through her intercession. St. Alphonsus Liguori, in his *Glories of Mary*, states, "It is the will of God that all graces should come to us through the hands of Mary," and, he theorizes, not only to those who pray to her, but even to those who forget her or deride her.

That last notion always amazes us Catholics. How could devotion to Mary take anything away from her Son? Instead it enhances His power and authority. That He could bring His lowly handmaiden to the summit of holiness, the highest and greatest that a mere creature can attain, is certainly to His credit and glory.

Since He has, in fact, done this, our only response must be to marvel at His work. And to respond in kind —if He has so praised her, we must imitate Him and praise her too. We honor her because He has honored her first.

The original feast of Our Lady of Grace was the Feast of the Visitation of Mary to Elizabeth. On that occasion she brought Divine Grace Himself to Elizabeth and Zachary and John the Baptizer. What an astounding meeting that was, when prompted by the Holy Spirit, Elizabeth and Zachary prophesied and the Baptizer was sanctified in his mother's womb.

"Treasurer of Jesus Christ," says St. Albert the Great, or, in the words of St. Peter Damian, "Treasurer of divine graces." St. Anselm calls Mary "the Mother of all graces," and St. Bernardine of Siena says that "all the gifts and graces we receive from God are dispensed by the hands of Mary."

Speaking of this power of Mary's mediation, the Second Vatican Council sees it as "a sharing in the one unique source that is the mediation of Christ himself." It continues, "The Church does not hesitate to profess this subordinate role of Mary. She experiences it continuously and commends it to the hearts of the faithful so that, encouraged by this maternal help, they may more closely adhere to the one Mediator and Redeemer."

Pope John Paul II states it in his Marian Year II encyclical, *Mother of the Redeemer*: "The Church knows and teaches with St. Paul that there is only one Mediator, 'for there is one God and there is one mediator between God and man, the man Christ Jesus, who gave himself as a ransom for all' (1 Tim 2:5-6). The maternal role of Mary towards people in no way obscures or diminishes the unique mediation of Christ, but rather shows its power: it is mediation in Christ."

After reviewing the work of the Incarnation and the role God assigned in it to Mary, the Holy Father concludes, "With the redeeming death of her Son, the maternal mediation of the handmaid of the Lord took on a universal dimension, for the work of redemption embraces the whole of humanity. Thus there is manifested in a singular way the efficacy of the one and universal mediation of Christ between God and man.

"Mary's cooperation shares, in its subordinate character, in the universality of the mediation of the Redeemer, the one Mediator." The character of this intercession was first manifested at Cana of Galilee. "In this way Mary's motherhood continues unceasingly in the Church as the mediation which intercedes and the Church expresses her faith in this truth by invoking Mary under the titles of Advocate, Auxiliatrix, Adjutrix and Mediatrix."

As we meditate on this Marian title, Mother of Divine Grace, it takes on new dimensions. How often we ask one another, "Pray for me"! And we take this request quite seriously. If we are ready to take on this office of mediation for one another, how much more seriously does the office suit the Blessed Mother!

The words of the *Memorare* help us express this confidence in her intercession:

Remember O most gracious Virgin Mary,
That never was it known,
That anyone who fled to your protection,
implored your help,
or sought your intercession,
Was left unaided.
Inspired by this confidence, we fly to your protection
O Virgin of virgins,
our Mother.
To you do we come, before you we kneel,
sinful and sorrowful,
O Mother of the Word Incarnate.
Despise not our petitions but in your mercy
Hear and answer me. Amen.

7

Mother Most Pure

The virtue of Mary that is honored in this title is her purity of heart, such as her Son expressed in the Beatitudes, "Blest are the pure in heart, for they shall see God" (Mt 5:8).

Our Lord is praising those who understood that the Levitical rituals of purification were meant to promote the inner conversion of heart that would free the soul from attachment to material goods and free it for spiritual perfection.

How often the prophets bemoaned the fact that the exterior service of God was accepted as an excuse for avoiding the inner, spiritual practice of religion. The scrupulous observances of the scribes and Pharisees earned warnings from Christ when they were a substitute for spiritual adherence to God.

He told His disciples that they must accept the Kingdom of God "as a little child," and He warned His followers to beware of "the leaven of the Pharisees." That must have come as a great shock to them, for they were the people's model for Jewish observances at the time.

This integrity of heart, the true purity, was certainly exemplified in Our Lady. Her holiness had no equal in any other mere human being. Pope Pius IX expresses it in this way: "It was right that, as the Only-Begotten had a Father in heaven whom the Seraphim proclaimed thrice holy, so He would have a Mother on the earth who should never lack the splendor of holiness."

He adds, she is "more beautiful than beauty, more gracious than grace, more holy than holiness, and alone holy, and most pure in soul and body, who has surpassed all perfection and all virginity, and has become the dwelling place of all the graces of the most Holy Spirit, and who, God alone excepted, is superior to all, and by nature fairer, more beautiful and more holy than the Cherubim and Seraphim; she whom all the tongues of heaven and earth do not suffice to extol."

Mary understood this purity of heart in the way Romano Guardini describes it in *The Lord*, "We must try to understand something of the uniqueness of the Sermon on the Mount: its revolutionary tidings; the energy with which it insists upon the progression from the outer, specific acts of virtue to the inner, all-permeating state of virtue; its demand for identification-of-self-with-neighbor as the sole measure of purity of intent, and consequently, its definition of love as the essence of man's new disposition."

The gospel records of Mary show how concerned she was for others, and how this translated into acts of charity. Whether it was to hasten to help St. Elizabeth, or cover the embarrassment of the newlyweds at Cana, Mary is there with the actions that show her interior disposition.

When we ask, "What did Jesus look like?" we have to answer "Just like his mother," for He took His entire human nature directly from her without benefit of male seed. And the reverse is true, Mary looked just like Jesus.

But if this pious observation has any meaning, it is more important to realize that as she helped form His human traits, so she was formed by her long years with Him. That she actually considered herself the little slave girl of the Lord (*ancilla domini*) tells us how seriously she sought to serve, and be like, her God.

Those years which we call the Hidden Life of our Lord were years at Nazareth when Mary learned from the very source of holiness what it meant to be a faithful follower, a real Christian.

Her purity of heart was learned in the midst of poverty, real poverty, the lack of many material possessions. She identified herself with the "people of the land," those who had learned to depend on and cling to God alone. In her triumphant canticle, she proclaims, "For he has looked upon his handmaid's lowliness. . ." (Lk 1:48).

In the beatitudes, Christ clearly shows the difference in the way the world looks at misfortune and the way God uses it for the purification of the soul and the ultimate reward. Mary would not have been envied by the wealthy and the powerful of her lifetime, but hers was the reflected glory from her Son which she would share for all eternity.

Chaplain Leo Sherely-Price, of the Royal Navy, writes in his book, *Queen of Peace*, "The blessing and promise of Our Lord to the 'pure in heart' comes to its fullest fruit and realization in Mary. It may well be that it was his Mother whom, above all, Jesus had in mind when he uttered these words on the Mount. . . ."

He goes on to say she "is the Rose of Sharon and Lily of the Valley of our exile. All her loveliness of soul, all her radiant purity comes, she tells us, from the love of God, and readily we beg her:

'Make me feel as you have felt,
Make my heart to glow and melt
With the love of Christ my Lord.'"

When Pope Paul VI journeyed to Nazareth in 1964, he caught the vision of the school of perfection that was the Holy Family that went on there for about thirty years. He said, "How I would like to return to my childhood and attend the simple yet profound school that is Nazareth! How wonderful to be close to Mary, learning again the lesson of the true meaning of life, learning again God's truths."

8

Mother Most Chaste

In his Gospel, St. John speaks sarcastically of Caiaphas, who was High Priest "for that year." The great dignity of the high priesthood was meant to be a lifetime office above and beyond political manipulation.

In today's world, the sanctity of marriage is attacked on all sides, and the lifetime vows, "until death do us part," are openly ridiculed in words and actions. "No fault" divorces are easier to obtain than no-fault insurance. In this title of the Litany, we not only salute the personal, bodily purity of the Blessed Mother, but we see her and St. Joseph as the models for the virtue of chastity for both the married and the single.

The Son of God took His flesh from Mary. It is impossible to think that He would have taken it from any but the purest and most precious of creatures. When the Church defined the privilege of Mary's Immaculate Conception in 1854, it proclaimed her perpetual sinlessness from the instant of her conception by St. Joachim and St. Ann.

This Immaculate Virgin was then chosen to be the Mother of the Incarnate Word whose own purity had foreordained His Mother's. As the ancient poet Cynewulf proclaimes: "Hail, you are the glory of this middle world, the purest woman throughout all the earth." She is, indeed, the purest creature ever created.

It is Catholic belief that Mary preserved this sinlessness throughout her life. It was a tremendous gift from God.

However, this is only the beginning of the story. On the positive side, Mary practiced all the virtues of her state in life to the highest degree. In this title of the Litany, we acknowledge her perfect chastity, that she kept herself from all sensual satisfaction.

To do this, St. Joseph would have had to be aware of her vow of virginity, accepted it, and practiced it himself. St. Bernard shows us the grave anxiety of Joseph when confronted with the pregnancy of his espoused wife, knowing that he was not the father. St. Bernard points out that only God's merciful action in sending the angel to Joseph could have calmed his doubts and allowed him to share in the work of our salvation.

St. Thomas Aquinas returns to this point several times in the *Summa*: "It is clear that perpetual virginity was an outstanding virtue in the Mother of God. It was fitting that her virginity be consecrated to God by vow." Then, "After her marriage to Joseph according to the customs of the time, they both took the vow of virginity." Finally, "After the espousal, Mary and Joseph both vowed absolute virginity."

St. Augustine tells us that "Joseph was her husband even though the marriage rights were not used. . . Joseph is listed to give due honor to the male sex which should never be separated from the lines of generation, but even more so, that he would never seem to be separated from the woman to whom he was joined in such affection of soul."

From St. Albert the Great we read, "We are told that St. Joseph was a carpenter, that he earned his bread by the skillful use of his hands, not eating the bread of leisure and delight, as the scribes and Pharisees did. Mary also was the busy housewife, a worker."

"What sort of a man Joseph was can easily be learned from the position he was deputized to take. He had the title 'Father' in relation to Christ, and, indeed, was believed to be the father by many at that time," writes St. Bernard. And he adds, "He is that good and faithful servant whom the Lord has put in charge of his household. He had the privilege of being the support of the Mother, the guardian of the Son, and the most trusted helper in God's plan for mankind."

The saints were fascinated with the question, "Why would the Virgin Mother need to enter into a marriage with St. Joseph?" The reasons they come up with include: in view of the Virgin Birth of Our Lord, to protect Mary's reputation from evil-minded people, to give her and the Christ Child the protection of Joseph, to provide Jesus legal right to the title "Son of David," to hide the mystery of the Virgin Birth until the proper time, to sanctify marriage and to glorify marriage. These last two reasons were considered of prime importance.

Whenever we consider the lives of Mary and Joseph, we see two people who are true models for all married people, save for their vows of virginity. But the chastity which is included in such a state is a model for all people.

The gift of human sexuality is a great gift from God, on the natural level. To protect it by chaste lives, according to our state in life, is our tribute to God for the gift and our way of thanking Him for it.

The example of the Holy Family has been most effective through the Christian centuries. Young people have kept themselves pure to prepare for marriage and to give *themselves* completely to their beloved spouses.

Men and women have embraced the religious life to proclaim to the world that God is the one love of their lives. Because sexuality is such a truly noble gift, their offer to make this sacrifice proclaims to the world that those who use it in marriage are living a good way of life.

Married people — using their gift to bring children into the world, to co-create with God, to foster their mutual love and to grow into a union of lifelong love with each other — witness by their marital chastity to the power of God's grace. And God has responded by making their way of life holy through the Sacrament of Matrimony.

The world, which ridicules the virtue of chastity,

has fallen victim to its own unrestrained lust. And what a false god that is! How quickly unruly sex betrays its followers! No slavery is so absolute as that of "free love."

The example of this most chaste woman, Virgin and Mother, is so needed in our world!

Or, as Pope Leo XIII wrote in 1892: "In truth, fathers of families have in Joseph the most glorious example of paternal vigilance and providence; mothers, in the most holy Virgin Mother of God, have the outstanding example of love, of modesty, of openness of mind and of perfect faith; and children of the family, in Jesus Who was subject to them, have the divine example of obedience, which they should admire, cultivate and imitate."

9

Mother Inviolate

In a work as devotional as the Litany of Loreto, many of the titles overlap, each bringing just a different shade of meaning, a subtle nuance, to the words of praise.

That Mary was "inviolate" is taken for granted. No taint or hint of sin ever touched her soul, yet she understood well the effects of sin from what her Son endured to pay the price for our redemption.

A mother does not have to have appendicitis to suffer along with a child who must go under the knife. And in this way, Mary the compassionate Mother has become indeed the Refuge of Sinners. She knows the terrible hurt, the awful pain, of sin.

St. Augustine's famous line tells us: "Concerning the Holy Virgin Mary, I wish no question to be raised at all when we are treating of sins."

Cardinal Newman refered to her in these words, "On the other hand, we admit, rather we maintain, that except for the grace of God, she might have sinned; and that she may have been exposed to temptation in the sense in which Our Lord was exposed to it, though as his divine Nature made it impossible for him to yield to it, so his grace preserved her under its assaults also."

St. Alphonsus is even more dramatic in his understanding of Mary's sinlessness and growth in sanctity in his book, *The Glories of Mary*: "From the first moment of her life she began to love God with all her strength and gave herself entirely to Him. . . She offered her entire self to God, wholly and without reserving anything — all her powers and all her senses, her whole mind and her whole heart, her whole soul and her whole body. . . ."

The Fathers of the Church loved to contrast Eve and Mary, playing on the word *Eva* transformed into

Ave! As Christ was the New Adam, Mary was considered the New Eve.

All that Eve could have become is found in its fullness in Mary. That is the significance of the message of Gabriel to her, summed up in that glorious *Ave!* at the Annunciation. It is no wonder that the Church applies to her the words, "Who is she that approaches as a brilliant dawn, fair as the moon, bright as the sun, terrible as an army drawn up in battle array."

St. Bernard exults, "Rejoice, O father Adam, and even more, rejoice and exult mother Eve. You, the first parents of all the living have unfortunately given life to mankind, tainted with sin. But now you can be comforted in your great daughter. O Eve, the shame that you have passed down to all women will now be taken away."

In his treatise against heresies, St. Irenaeus proclaims, "Eve responded by falling away from God. Mary's obedience to the angelic message brought God into her womb. Eve listened and lost God; Mary listened and obeyed God. The Virgin Mary has become the advocate of the virgin Eve. . . Mary's obedience has finally balanced the debt of disobedience."

"Eve mourned but Mary exulted," writes St. Augustine. "Eve carried tears in her womb; Mary carried joy. Eve gave birth to a sinner; Mary gave us the Innocent One. From Eve came sin; from Mary grace. . . The faith and obedience of Mary compensate for the pride and disobedience of Eve."

As always, a true devotion to Mary, a deeper understanding of her role in the economy of salvation leads us to a greater appreciation for and love of her Son.

The enmity between the devil and the Woman promised in the protevangelium (Gen 3:6-16) continues to this day and for all time. We confidently expect Mary's intercession for all sinners in their time of need and especially at the hour of death. With that certitude we conclude the Hail Mary over and over again, "Pray for us sinners, now and at the hour of our death."

As St. Alphonsus remarks, "Recourse to Mary is a most secure means to conquer all the assaults of hell." And he adds, "For this reason Mary is said to be terrible as an army in battle array." St. Bonaventure agrees with him by writing: "O how fearful is Mary to the devils!"

We have already quoted at length the passage from St. Bernard where he tells us that in all our trials and difficulties, we should look up to the Star, look to Mary.

The great Eastern Father, St. John Damascene, in commenting on the Annunciation, asserts that "While I keep my hope in you unconquerable, O Mother of God, I shall be safe. I will fight and overcome my enemies with no other buckler than your protection and your all-powerful aid."

We know that this title, "Mother Inviolate," is a glorious tribute to her perpetual virginity and her perpetual sinlessness, but we can see in it, too, the Woman who conquered Satan; the Mother of God who, victorious over all evil, would help us, too, to triumph over sin.

We know that there is no more certain way to obtain divine help from Christ than through the intercession of His Mother. How often we pay tribute to this belief in our prayer, the *Salve Regina*:

Hail Holy Queen, Mother of Mercy! Hail our life, our sweetness, and our hope! To you do we cry, poor banished children of Eve; to you do we send up our sighs, mourning and weeping in this valley of tears! Turn then, most gracious advocate, your eyes of mercy toward us; and after this, our exile, show unto us the blessed fruit of your womb, Jesus, O clement, O loving, O sweet Virgin Mary!

10

Mother Undefiled

The Latin word, *intemerata*, which is used to describe this attribute in Our Lady, has the meaning of being supremely sinless, uncorrupted, and not so much as touched by even the slightest stain of sin.

It is probably used in the sense in which Holy Scripture uses it. "Religion that is pure and undefiled before God and the Father is this: to visit orphans and widows in their affliction; and to keep oneself unstained by the world" (Jas 1:27).

In speaking of Christ, the author of Hebrews writes, "It was fitting that we should have such a high priest: holy, innocent, undefiled, separated from sinners, higher than the heavens" (Heb 7:26).

Many verses of the Song of Songs, attributed to Solomon, are applied to the Blessed Mother both in the liturgy and in devotional literature. One that probably influenced this title is "Open to me, my sister, my beloved, my dove, my perfect (undefiled) one" (Sg 5:2).

With all this emphasis on the utter sinlessness of Mary, we might wonder if she distances herself from the sinner as much as she distances herself from sin.

Christian devotion unanimously shows she reacts with just the opposite attitude. Because she is sinless, Mary knows how wretched those are who live in sin.

Pope St. Gregory VII formulates this beautifully: "The higher and holier she is, the greater is her sweetness and compassion towards sinners, who have recourse to her with the desire to amend their lives."

And, with accustomed boldness, St. Bernard adds, "Why should human frailty fear to go to Mary? In her there is no austerity, nothing terrible: she is all sweetness, offering help to all."

The first reason for the great love that Mary has for

us is the great love that she has for God. Love towards God and love towards our neighbor belong to the same commandment. "This is the commandment we have from him: whoever loves God must also love his brother" (1 Jn 4:21).

There are no limits to what the saints have done for their neighbor, motivated by the love of God. Examine the life of St. Francis Xavier, St. Francis de Sales, St. Isaac Jogues, St. Maximilian Kolbe, and other recent heroes such as Father Damien, the leper. I marvel at the life of Padre Junipero Serra who gave himself unsparingly for his Indians. And the examples could be multiplied over and over again.

Mary, the chosen heroine of God's grace, could do no less. Because all of the human race has been redeemed by Jesus, her Son, she loves and intercedes for them all.

Anyone born a Catholic and who is now of mature years has heard those medieval legends about Mary helping sinners in through the back door of Heaven, or over the walls, etc. These myths are offensive to pious ears.

They try to make of Jesus a just and unbending Judge, while Mary embodies the mercy of God. Ridiculous! Jesus shows Himself as the Good Shepherd, anxious to gather in sinners. He ate with publicans and sinners because they needed the divine Physician more than the righteous needed Him. He is our Holy Redeemer who gave His life for us, the innocent for the sinner.

As Therese of Lisieux remarks, "the justice of God works more mightily for us than the mercy of God."

Mary's intercession is always "in Jesus," reflecting the mercy and patience and love that she sees there. She whose will was so perfectly in tune with the will of God has not changed with her entrance into heaven. In his *Glories of Mary*, St. Alphonsus Liguori uses part of his first chapter to emphasize that Mary shows herself a Mother most effectively for *repentant* sinners.

He writes, "Whoever aspires to be a child of this great Mother must first abandon sin, and then may hope to be accepted as such." And again, "If a sinner, though he may not yet have given up his sin, endeavors to do so, and for this purpose seeks the help of Mary, this good Mother will not fail to assist him" and, by her intercession, help him recover the grace of God.

Obstinacy in sin would certainly make a mockery of anyone who wanted to be, or claimed to be, a child of Mary. Mary welcomes sinners who are sincerely repentant and who need her help on their road back to God. Such a one she cannot and will not refuse!

In the private revelations that Mary has granted, her constant refrain is "Repent and follow my Son." This echoes her "Whatever my Son tells you to do, do" at Cana, her last recorded words in the Gospels.

At Lourdes, her constant refrain to St. Bernardette was "Repentance, repentance, repentance." She complained of the impiety of Christians, the coldness of those who should know and love.

At LaSalette she urged this on the two children, and at Fatima she repeated it to the three youngsters. As current as this writing, Our Lady seems to be making the same plea at Medjugorje in Yugoslavia. Her message there is very forthright:

"Return to the ways of God and convert your lives to peace with God and your fellow men."

This woman, so totally unspoiled, so precious to God, is described by the theologian Karl Adam in his *Spirit of Catholicism*: "Mary's importance in the work of salvation does not lie chiefly in the purely bodily sphere, but in the sphere of morality and religion.

"It consists in this, that Mary, so far as lay in her, gave the best of herself, even her whole being, to the service of God, and that, however infinitely small all human doing and suffering are in comparison with the Divine Perfection, she surrendered this infinitely small without limitation or stint to the visitation of Divine

Grace, and so prepared herself to be the sublime instrument of the divine work of redemption."

For this Marian title, St. Alphonsus composed this prayer: "O my immaculate Queen, fair dove and the beloved of God, look on the many stains and wounds of my soul: see me and have pity on me. God, who loves you so much, denies nothing to you, and you never refuse to assist those who have recourse to you. O Mother inviolate, pray for us."

11

Mother Most Lovable
(Mother Most Amiable)
(Dearest of Mothers)

In order to be loved, a person must be loved, and artists throughout the ages have recognized this quality in the Blessed Mother. They have depicted her in all of her various mysteries, from the Annunciation to the Assumption, from the Immaculate Conception to her Coronation in heaven, but the title *Mater Amabilis* has inspired more people than any other title.

"Deep waters cannot quench love," sings the Wise Man, "nor floods sweep it away" (Sg 8:7). And Maccabees is even more specific about maternal love: "Most admirable and worthy of everlasting remembrance was the mother, who saw her seven sons perish in a single day, yet bore it courageously because of her hope in the Lord" (2 Mcc 7:20).

In the New Testament, Christ summed up His whole moral code in the Law of Love, and His beloved disciple states it quite simply, "Let us love one another because love is of God. . ." (1 Jn 4:7).

In Mary, the devout Christian sees the summit of God's love expressed in a mere creature. Mary is the beloved of God, Father, Son and Holy Spirit.

She is the beloved of St. Joseph and of all the saints. She is truly the dearest of Mothers to us Christians.

The graces with which God adorned her soul are without peer among all the creation of which we are aware. The Father created her to be His perfect Daughter and gave her as sublime a vocation as can be imagined. She was created to be the worthy Mother of

His Son. St. Alphonsus comments, "Mary was so beautiful in the eyes of God that he was enamored of her beauty." No wonder the Church often applies this phrase from the Song of Songs to her, "How beautiful you are, my love, how beautiful you are!" (4:1).

Mary was lovable to Jesus simply because she was His Mother. All her dignity, all her glory, every privilege she has, is traced directly to that fact, the divine maternity. In the divine plan of the Incarnation, Mary was necessary, because God willed it so.

He willed that it be a perfect mother-son relationship. She wasn't used simply to provide Jesus with His human nature, a physical body. She was needed to nurse Him and nurture Him, to teach Him and form Him.

It was the will of God that she be present at Bethlehem, Nazareth, Cana of Galilee, the Cenacle, Calvary, Easter, and Pentecost. "The mother of Jesus was there" (Jn 2:1).

No one ever outgrows his mother, even if it is considered overdone if this is trumpeted about in public. No one ever wants to be smothered by her, yet we always want her approval. The force of mother love is a universal example in our human affairs.

If this is true of our weak human nature, it was even more evident in the relationship of Jesus and Mary. His first public miracle was worked through her intercession at Cana; she stood by Him on Calvary, and He made provision for her care by St. John at that solemn hour.

When a woman from the crowd cried out, "Blessed is the womb that bore you and the breasts that nourished you," Christ immediately raised that praise to a higher level, "Rather, blessed are those who hear the word of God and keep it" (Lk 11:27-28).

Blessed as Mary was because of her physical relationship to Christ, her spiritual love for Him brought her to ever greater heights.

Mary learned her holiness through her close association with Christ from the very beginning of His earthly life. She was the First Christian, the first to draw from the infinite treasury of the love who was her Son. It is holiness which makes a creature most like God, and Mary, being His most holy creation, is the most like God of all of us human beings.

Holiness is always a magnet. It attracts people to find that peace and joy in the Lord. We see it in the faces and the behavior of those who have found Christ, and it is attractive. Mary, who lived always in the presence of God, was most lovable, radiating that Christ-like presence.

As one who was full of grace, Mary's soul was the delight of the Holy Spirit. He had graced her with all of His gifts and fruits so that she was totally in tune with the will of God. Her *fiat* was the culmination of that grace and the doorway to ever more grace.

When St. Therese of Lisieux was worried about the souls in heaven having different rewards, her sister placed three jars of different sizes before her. She told the girl to fill each one. Then Therese tells us that she could see that each one was as full as it was possible for it to be.

This is true of the Blessed Mother. As her relationship with Christ grew through the years, she grew spiritually and was able to have ever more grace.

It is most appropriate that we also comment on the love that St. Joseph had for his wife, the Blessed Virgin. The fact that it was a virginal marriage does not mean that it was a cold arrangement. Passion is not necessary to love, nor are bodies. The romance of Mary and Joseph drew its strength from their holiness, their relationship to Christ.

St. Teresa of Avila, that great Doctor of prayer, tells us about her experience when she first started having devotion to St. Joseph. "I am quite amazed when I consider the great favors our Lord has shown to me through the intercession of this blessed saint, and the many dangers both of body and soul from which he has delivered me."

The holiness of Mary and Joseph started with their relationship in the Holy Family to the Christ Child as they nurtured Him through the silent years at Nazareth.

The lovableness, the amiability, of Mary, is put in dry, but exact theological perspective by St. Thomas Aquinas: "The Blessed Virgin Mary is said to have merited the privilege of bearing the Lord of all, not because it was through her merits that He became Incarnate, but because by the grace bestowed upon her she merited that measure of purity and holiness which fitted her to be the Mother of God."

No wonder then that the whole Christian world sings forth her praises. This lovable Mother has been the patroness of countless cathedrals, basilicas, monasteries, convents, parish churches and various institutions. She has been the inspiration that brings loving beauty to the world.

Artists, poets, composers and all the saints are troubadours of Mary. St. Bernard, in fact, has been given the title, "Troubadour of Mary." In this Litany, we are given the opportunity to add our voices to theirs. What a privilege!

12

Mother Most Admirable
(Model of Motherhood)
(Mother Most Wonderful)

When the Archangel Gabriel appeared to the prophet Daniel, he promptly fainted away. The stories run throughout the Bible of the reaction of men and women in the presence of the supernatural, especially angels. The sense of awe and wonder that Moses felt in the presence of the burning bush that was not consumed belongs to this order.

Mary, as the admirable, wonderful Mother, leaves us with this same impression. He who is mighty has done great things in her soul and has given her the highest vocation that mere humanity could aspire to, the work of being the Mother of God.

There is almost a fairy tale simplicity to this story. The little maiden of Nazareth, identifying herself with the poor people of the land, hardly worthy to be considered a slave-girl in God's camp, is suddenly exalted to a position above the angels.

Because we want to share this feeling, we go off on pilgrimage to places that have a special religious significance for us.

When the pilgrims enter the shrine at Guadalupe in Mexico City, there is an almost palpable feeling of the sanctity of the place. I felt the same thing at the Shrine of St. Anne-de-Beaupre in Quebec, and even more so when I traced the sacred places in the Holy Land.

There is a feeling of wonder, of awe, of awareness that God has been active here in a special way.

The home of the Holy Family in Nazareth was truly a model for all family living. In St. Joseph we see a worthy model for fathers, in Mary, a true role-model for mothers, and in the Christ Child, an example for all growing children and teenagers.

St. Bernard has a lengthy meditation on this in his first *Missus Est* homily. He is commenting on Luke 2:51, " 'He went down with them and came to Nazareth and was obedient to them. . . .'

"And He was subject to them. Who? And to whom? God was subject to man! God, I repeat, to whom the angels are subject, whom Principalities and Powers obey, was subject to Mary, and not only to Mary, but to Joseph, too, because of Mary.

"Wonder, indeed, at both, but choose which is the more wonderful. Is it that most loving condescension of the Son, or the tremendous dignity of the Mother? Both are astounding, both miraculous.

"God submitting in obedience to a woman is indeed humility without equal; the woman commanding her God is sublime above measure. In praising virgins we read that they follow the Lamb wherever he goes. How can he possibly praise enough the Virgin who leads him?

"Learn, O man, to obey. Learn, O earth, to be subject. Learn, O dust, to bow down. In speaking of our Creator the Evangelist says, 'And He was subject to them,' that is, to Mary and Joseph."

Further on, St. Bernard continues, "If you cannot follow him wherever he goes, then at least deign to follow him when he humbles himself for you. If you cannot follow the sublime pathways of virginity, at least follow that safest of pathways, humility. Whoever strays from this path, no matter how virginal he may be, will certainly not follow the Lamb wherever he goes . . . .

"The sinful man who chooses to follow in humility has a much safer path than the proud man who tries to follow in virginity. Humble reparation cleanses the former, even as pride spoils the cleanness of the other.

"But Mary is truly blessed, for in her, neither virginity nor humility are lacking in any way. Hers is a singular virginity which does not fear child-bearing, but rather honors it. She is also endowed with the humility equal to this sublime task. Which of these virtues is more admirable, more incomparable?"

And he concludes by exclaiming, "O all you angels and saints, honor the Mother of the King you adore, for He made Himself subject to her!"

Five centuries before this, St. Sophronius of Jerusalem wrote in wonder at Mary's prerogatives, "No one has ever been raised to such heights of magnificence as you. Never before was there one who shone so brightly with heavenly light, who was so exalted above all the heavens.

"And rightly so, for no one has ever been so close to God as you. On no one has God ever bestowed the gifts he has given you. No one but you has been so full a participant in God's grace."

We must marvel at this woman whose will was so in tune with the will of God. Sanctity for all mankind lies in that direction.

St. Ignatius Loyola teaches this in his famous prayer. "Take, O Lord, and receive all my liberty, my memory, my understanding, my will. All that I have or am is yours, and I return it to you to be disposed of according to your will. Give me only your love and your grace and I am amply rich. I can desire nothing more."

St. John of the Cross, the great Carmelite mystic, expresses it in this way: "The state of divine union consists in the total transformation of the will into the will of God."

When we recognize how fully this was applied in Mary's life, we have cause to wonder, to stand in awe. Mary is, for the Christian, the mother to whom we turn for instruction, for guidance, for enlightenment, for direction in pursuing the will of God. She is the most perfect example of the life of grace.

The artist has captured that in the picture, "Mater Admirabilis," a fresco in the Sacred Heart Convent of the Trinita dei Monti in Rome. He pictures her as a child in the Temple, resting from her task of spinning. He painted her with a wonderful attitude of modesty and recollection, which are external signs of the interior union with God. Everything points to the fact that she is enjoying the presence of God.

The essential joy of heaven is to see God face to face, to know Him even as we are known. But we hope, also, to enjoy such concomitant glories as the companionship of His most blessed Mother. We want to be immersed in the wonderful presence of God's love and what it has effected in her, His choicest creation.

13
Mother of Good Counsel

There are some people who brush aside all mention of the miraculous as if it couldn't happen. They act as if God, the Supreme Lawgiver, cannot rise above the laws of nature He has established.

So, at the legends of the saints they smile condescendingly. The stories of statues and pictures, especially in Italy, that respond in any way are just too much for these sophisticated people.

They balk at such simple stories as that told of St. Bernard — that every time he passed a picture or statue of Mary, he murmured a fervent little, "Ave, Maria!" and one day she responded, "Ave, Bernarde!"

These people lose a great deal of the richness of Catholic living, wherein God is always just a prayer away and very understanding of our little human needs and loves. They are unaware of how all-embracing God's love is for His "little ones." And aren't we all children of God from the youngest and most simple to those learned people with doctorates and sophisticated attitudes?

The story of the famous, and beautiful, picture of Our Lady of Good Counsel falls into this category.

There is a little town in Italy, a bit southeast of Rome, called Genezzano. In pagan times it housed a famous shrine to Venus, but in the fourth century a church was established there under the title of the Virgin Mother of Good Counsel.

It had an honorable life of service, but by the fifteenth century it had fallen into disrepair. A pious woman of the area gave all she had to restore the church.

Meanwhile, there was a little church in Scutari, Albania, dedicated to the Annunciation, which contained a very ancient, "miraculous" picture of the Blessed Mother. As the Turkish Moslems advanced and threatened the destruction of the Catholics in the area, plans were made to remove the picture to a safe place.

Suddenly, the picture was enveloped in a white cloud and carried, as if by unseen hands, to the restored church at Genezzano on Sunday, April 25, 1467. Music accompanied the event, and the church bells throughout the town started ringing by themselves.

The picture was placed in the chapel of St. Blaise and the people responded with great fervor to "the Madonna from Paradise." The chapel and the picture were soon referred to by the title of the Church, Our Lady of Good Counsel.

Several popes put their seal of approval on this devotion, notably Innocent XI, Benedict XIV, Pius IX and Leo XIII. Leo XIII kept a copy of the picture on his desk, and inscribed a copy of it with "My son, listen to her counsels." He added the title, Mother of Good Counsel, to the Litany in 1903.

In these days when there is so much unrest in the world, how deeply we need the good advice, the right guidance, of the Blessed Mother. We are told that Europe is in a "post-Christian" mode and that in a nominally Catholic country such as France, only about 4% of the people attend Mass regularly.

The big worldly powers are stockpiling nuclear weapons at a deadly rate, and we are told they can destroy the world a hundred times over. World leaders need all the guidance that they can get to work effectively for peace.

The poor, the hungry, the homeless who roam the big cities, the deprived who struggle for survival in the Third World, the dangers from imperial Communism, the perils to the ecology — you can name these distressing problems and more. As the planet Earth rapidly becomes the world village, we hear more and more that makes us apprehensive. To whom shall we turn to intercede for us at the Throne of God, if not Mary, our Mother of Good Counsel. As we pray in the *Salve Regina*, she is our "most gracious advocate."

Her Son was hailed by Isaiah the Prophet in this way: "For a Child is born to us, and a Son is given to us, and the government is upon his shoulder: his Name shall be called, Wonderful, Counselor, God the mighty, the Father of the World to come, the Prince of Peace" (9:6).

His is the wisdom so greatly needed in the world today. His is the voice that alone can proclaim the way to peace. His is the only message that promises help to a troubled world.

Mary, the Mother of this Counselor, has such great power with Him. We beg her to plead with Him that leaders and nations and individuals will look to His example and turn from their inhumane ways.

Our Lord promised, before He finished His earthly career, that He would send us "another advocate, the paraclete," and we know that He fulfilled this promise on the original Feast of Christian Pentecost.

He poured forth His Holy Spirit on the world to be our advocate, our counselor. He promised that this Spirit of Truth would be with His Church to the end of time.

Mary, who conceived by the Holy Spirit, has been a special vessel of His election and a sure channel of the graces He dispenses. We must turn to her and ask that she intercede with Him to send forth those all consuming flames of love to conquer the coldness of modern man and the shadow of death under which we live.

And in our personal lives, this title of Mary has special meaning, too. Whenever a person has to go to court, we always ask, "Do you have a good lawyer, a good counselor?" In other countries, the question may be phrased as "Do you have a good advocate?"

For each of us, the certitude of death is inescapable. When we appear before the judgment seat of a God who is both merciful and just, who will be our lawyer? Who will plead our case with urgency and concern? Who will be the advocate for the defense?

It is no wonder that, when our life is over, and only the angels can count how many times we have recited the "Hail Mary," its final phrase will have so much importance for us:

"Pray for us sinners, now and at the hour of our death. Amen."

14

Mother of Our Creator

The God whom earth and sea and sky
Adore and laud and magnify,
Whose might they own, whose praise they tell,
In Mary's body deigned to dwell.

O Mother blest! the chosen shrine
Wherein the Architect divine,
Whose hand contains the earth and sky,
Vouchsafed in hidden guise to lie.

Blest in the message Gabriel brought;
Blest in the work the Spirit wrought;
Most blest, to bring to human birth
The long desired of all the earth.

St. Venantius Fortunatus (A.D. 530-609) penned
these words in praise of Mary, the Mother of the
Creator, and the Church has us sing it at Morning
Prayer in the Liturgy of the Hours for feasts of Our
Lady.

Nevertheless, despite its antiquity, this title applied
to Our Lady is probably the most bold and forthright of
any words of faith. It must be understood, right from
the start, that these words are not pious exaggerations,
nor the flowery language of love.

They are based solidly on the doctrine of the Incarnation and our belief in the Holy Trinity. This Jesus,
who was born of Mary, is the second person of the
Blessed Trinity, therefore by nature God, and all creation comes from God. Works of creation can be attributed to Him.

This humble maiden, who is a creature, has the
relationship of "mother" to Him who is the creator of

the universe. In this sense it is true to call her the Mother of the Creator.

If it is theologically correct to call Mary the Mother of God, as was established by the Council of Ephesus, it is equally correct to call her the Mother of our Creator.

Now some non-Catholics object that this is giving praise to her above God, or in place of God. Nothing could be farther from the meaning of this title as the Church understands it and applies it to Mary. In fact, every Catholic child knows that Mary is a creature, but what a special relationship God the Creator wished to bestow on her!

In view of this relationship, Mary deserves these titles, as long as they are properly understood. Mother of the Creator does not imply in any way that Mary preceded God, or that she gave birth to the Divinity of God.

With that clearly understood, we can look at the many ways the Church uses this title in the liturgy. "Blessed are you, O Virgin Mary," we sing, in a typical passage, "who bore the Creator of all. You brought forth Him who made you and remained a virgin forever."

And in the Ambrosian hymn, *Jesu Redemptor Omnium*, we cry out, "Remember, O Creator of the word, that in being born you assumed the form of our body from the sacred womb of a Virgin."

An ancient antiphon, *O Admirabile Commercium*, states this clearly, "O admirable exchange, the Creator of the human race taking a living body, deigned to be born of a Virgin."

The hymn at the beginning of this chapter is another typical piece used to praise Mary.

The saints loved this title and appreciated its richness. St. Augustine reminds us that Jesus is "the Son by whom the world was made." And he continues, "The prophets sang that the Creator of heaven and earth would be on earth with men; the Angel announced that the Creator of flesh and spirit would come in the flesh."

St. Ephrem poses these rhetorical questions, "Who else lulled a Son in her bosom as Mary did? Who ever dared to call her son, Son of the Maker, Son of the Creator, Son of the Most High?" and he has Mary think, "The Babe that I carry carries me!"

In writing about the Nativity, St. Leo the Great tells us: "Today the Creator of the world is brought forth from the virginal womb, and he who made all natures is made the Son of her whom he created." Mary, Mother of the Creator? It could not be stated more definitely.

St. Ignatius Loyola states it more succinctly in the *Spiritual Exercises*: "Then her Creator became her Child." Mary, in fact, is the Masterpiece of God's Creation!

When we think of God the Creator, we can be lost in awe. As Abbot Columba Marmion remarks, "When we speak of divinity we can only lisp." God drew all creation out of nothing, *ex nihilo*, as the theologians remark. How stark, how majestic, the opening words of the Bible: "In the beginning God created. . . ."

The Creator of the starry heights, He who formed worlds and stars, galaxies and the universe, is viewed with wonder. Yet, His creation of man and angels, His closeness to them and His greater marvels in the work of Salvation, are all hinted at in the title we give Him, Creator.

His works of grace far exceed the worlds which came forth at His single word. And the Creator created Mary to be the centerpiece of that creation. No relationship between Creator and creature can be greater.

Dante, who was a fine theologian himself, almost the poetic echo of Aquinas, puts these words into the mouth of St. Bernard:

O Virgin Mother, daughter of your Son!
Created beings all in lowliness
Surpassing, as in height above them all;

Term by the Eternal Counsel preordained,
Ennobler of your nature, so advanced
In you, that its great maker did not scorn,
To make himself his own creation.

15

Mother of Our Savior
(Mother of Our Redeemer)

Father Hugh Blunt calls this invocation "Mary's most intimate title." With a little thought, the imposing moment of that statement becomes obvious.

Mary was the Mother of Jesus, who saved us from our sins, the Mother of Him who redeemed the whole human race, actual and potential. If there are rational beings on other planets and solar systems, not an outrageous thought, their economy of salvation will no doubt be different from ours.

For us, Jesus Christ is the Son of God and Savior. He came into the world through the Virgin Mary, not as some mere channel to provide Him a body and then be cast aside, but as His Mother.

She was with Him from Bethlehem to the Cenacle, from Cana to Calvary, from Easter to Pentecost. She was caught up, by divine decree, with His saving work from the time God prepared her soul at her Immaculate Conception, until she stood at the foot of the Cross, uniting her offering to His.

Because she was at the heart of the economy of salvation, because God sent the archangel Gabriel to obtain her *fiat*, she was an integral part of the plan.

St. Bernard understood this well since he proposes the rhetorical question, "Suppose she had said 'No!' " Would we still be waiting for the Messiah. Would Jesus still be the One who is to come?

St. Alphonsus Liguori understood this so well that he does not hesitate to call her "the Mediatrix" of our salvation, following the praise given her by St. Bonaventure. Understood in her being called into the economy of salvation, and granted that her consent was necessary, she joins her Son in the work of salvation.

Therefore, St. John Damascene says that "in a certain manner she can be called the savior of the world," so close is her relationship to Christ, our Holy Redeemer. By the consent she gave, according to St. Bernardine of Siena, "she procured us salvation."

Again, a caution is voiced. To praise God for His work in associating Mary so closely to the work of our redemption does not set Mary up on a plane with God! Mary also needed redemption. She, too, needed the price of salvation that her Son paid on Golgotha. Although Mary made no direct contribution to our redemption, she was vitally associated with her Son when He did this work. We must never forget the way St. John Damascene expressed Mary's contribution to our redemption was "in a certain way. . . ."

St. Thomas Aquinas tells us how Mary made the Incarnation possible: "He needed to be a man in order to be able to make satisfaction; and he needed to be God in order that, having alone power over the whole human race, he might be able to make satisfaction for humanity."

God asked Mary to be the Mother, not the producer. And with St. Bernard we too cry out, "O Virgin, quickly give your reply, give the word which earth, hell and even heaven itself awaits!"

Like all devout Jews, she yearned for the Messiah to come and set Israel free. Knowing the prophecies so well, she knew that it would be a mighty work, but one with great sorrow involved. Yet, she was so holy, so in tune with the will of God, so flexible to the workings of the Holy Spirit that she consented. While she did not merit the Incarnation, so holy was she that she merited that it would be accomplished through her.

The love that she lavished on her Son during his earthly career continues for the children He has redeemed throughout the rest of time. Christ is our Brother as well as our Redeemer and we too have been given into the tender maternal charity of Mary, His Mother.

Pope John Paul II makes the words of Vatican II's *Lumen Gentium* (No. 62) his own in the encyclical *Redemptoris Mater* (No. 40): "In this way Mary's motherhood continues unceasingly in the Church as the mediation which intercedes, and the Church expresses her faith in this truth by invoking Mary 'under the titles of Advocate, Auxiliatrix, Adjutrix and Mediatrix.'"

When we speak of her maternal care, another level of thought occurs. Mary is the Mother of the crucified Savior. When we look beyond the facts of Bethlehem, the great price of our salvation was worked out through the terrors and horrors of the Passion and Death.

Crucifixion was a terrible thing. It was designed to be a prolonged, torturous death to deter slaves from rebelling. Christ's perfect human nature underwent every possible height and depth of that pain and sorrow. No other human being ever suffered so much, so deeply, so exquisitely.

And Mary was there, standing at the foot of the cross, suffering with Him as only a mother can suffer. She joined in His offering of Himself to the Father, so perfectly was she in accord with the will of God.

How fitting then, that we can turn to her in our sorrows and sufferings, our everyday crosses, the duties of our state in life, and expect to be understood and helped. In our sorrows, our pains, our temptations, we can, with St. Bernard, "Look up to the Star, call upon Mary!"

Bossuet tells us that Mary's dignity as Mother of God assures her of the highest of places in heaven, "and the same Mary, being our Mother, makes her bend very low to us, to pity our weakness and to interest herself in our happiness."

Because Mary is the Mother of our Holy Redeemer, we must remember that she is the Mother of Him who freed us from the slavery of sin. To put that in a positive way, Christ Jesus is the one who liberated us, won for us the great gift of spiritual freedom.

Jesus and Mary were very familiar with the concept of slavery. The Roman Empire was built on a slave economy which was just as horrible as the slavery experienced by the Israelites in ancient Egypt, or the Negroes in the United States.

We are told that the American Indians never accepted slavery. They would simply allow themselves to be beaten to death rather than be enslaved.

Slavery of any sort is abhorrent, since God has given us the gift of freedom. God created us to be free, and our souls just simply yearn for that gift.

If physical freedom is so important, spiritual freedom is much more so. Slavery to sin, just because it can't be seen, is more of an aberration than physical slavery. In fact, the saints have likened it to physical leprosy or cancer, but again, a much higher disorder.

Christ our Redeemer, our Savior, is also truly our great Liberator. In all of this work, He willed that Mary be His associate.

The Church sings her praises under this title in one of the great concluding antiphons for the Liturgy of the Hours, the *Alma Redemptoris Mater*:

O Loving Mother of the Redeemer,
gate of heaven, star of the sea,
assist your people who have fallen yet strive to rise again.
To the wonderment of nature you bore your Creator,
yet remained a virgin after as before.
You who received Gabriel's joyful greeting,
have pity on us poor sinners.

16

Mother of the Church

This eloquent title, recently added to the Litany, actually embraces an ancient title deeply engraved in the Scriptures. Mary is the Mother of Christ who is the Head of the Body, His Church. Since she is the Mother of the Head of the Church, she is also the Mother of the Church, the Body of Christ.

Christ did not write a single book, or any part of a book, in the New Testament. That He did establish a church is obvious from Mt 16:18, Col 1:18, Eph 5:23 and almost one hundred other references to "church" or "churches" in the New Testament.

By the time of the death of the last Apostle, St. John, we had ample evidence that this church was highly visible, highly organized, unified and hierarchical. It was brought to life by the Holy Spirit, but it was not a simple, pious collection of any individuals who wanted to call themselves a church.

St. Ignatius of Antioch, the Bishop of Antioch who was martyred in A.D. 110, gives ample evidence to the organization of the Church of Christ as the Apostles left it.

In writing to St. Polycarp about his impending martyrdom, St. Ignatius says, "I offer myself up for those who obey the bishop, priests and deacons. . . ." Writing to the Ephesians, he says, "You must be made holy in all things by being united in perfect obedience, in submission to the bishop and the priests."

He is even more explicit in his letter to the Philadelphians. "Be careful, therefore, to take part in the one Eucharist for there is only one Flesh of our Lord Jesus Christ, and one cup to unite us with his Blood, one altar and one bishop, with the priests and deacons who are his fellow servants. Then, whatever you do you will do according to God. . . As sons of the light of truth, flee divisions and evil doctrines."

Listen to his words to the Trallians: "All should respect deacons as Jesus Christ, just as all should regard the bishop as the image of the Father, and the clergy as God's senate and the college of the Apostles. Without these three orders you cannot begin to speak of a church." He develops this theme further in the letter.

Note well that at the end of the apostolic era, the Church was left with a firm foundation of one bishop, surrounded by the priests, and served by the deacons.

If there are any individual things that the earliest Church Fathers attest to unanimously, their understanding of the organization of the visible Church, their belief in the Real Presence of Christ in the Eucharist, and their faith in the bodily resurrection of Christ, the God-Man, would have to tie for first place.

These things are the stumbling blocks to ecumenism in our times, but they do not allow for compromise. This is the Catholic Church of Christ that we proclaim in the title of Mary as Mother of the Church.

Modern devotion to Mary under this title begins with the proclamation by Pope Paul VI on November 21, 1964, in his concluding address to the third session of the Second Vatican Council:

"We declare most holy Mary Mother of the Church, that is of the whole Christian people, both faithful and pastors, who call her a most loving Mother; and we decree that henceforth the whole Christian people should, by this most sweet name, give still greater honor to the Mother of God and address prayers to her."

The Holy Father stressed the logical link as the close relationship between Mary and the Church. This is based on the fact that Christ, by His very Incarnation, was the Head of the Church.

"Mary is the Mother of Christ who, immediately

that he assumed human nature in her virginal womb, became the Head of his Mystical Body which is the Church. Mary, therefore, as Mother of Christ is to be considered as Mother also of all the faithful and pastors, that is, of the Church."

The pope refers to several of his predecessors who taught this same devotion to Mary, such as Pope Leo XIII, Pope Benedict XV and Pope St. Pius X. Pope John XXIII used the title at least five times.

The idea supporting this Marian title was summed up by St. Augustine: "Mary is truly Mother of the members of Christ which is what we are, because she cooperated by charity so that when the faithful should be born in the Church, who would be members of the Head, she herself being truly, in the body, Mother of the Head himself."

A little-known author in the twelfth century, Berengaud, seems to have the honor of being the first to use the title explicitly, *Mater Ecclesiae*. By the next century, the title started to gain some popularity, from the Cistercians at Solesme, St. Albert the Great, and in an old Irish litany.

While never a very popular title, it did begin to have minor usage from that time on.

There seems to be no doubt that Pope Paul VI intended that the title Mother of the Church should be the popular way to sum up the spirit of the Second Vatican Council. It was as if he put the implementation of the Council under her special patronage.

Two of the major solemn constitutions of Vatican II relate directly to the nature of the Church. They are *Lumen Gentium* and *Gaudium et Spes*. The other two, on divine Revelation and the Liturgy, certainly deal with the foundation of the Church and its spiritual apostolate.

The nine decrees that chart the direction of the Church in our times concern such important activities as priestly formation, the commission of bishops and priests and the immensely important one on the laity which has restored so many of their ministries.

Of the three declarations, the one on Religious Freedom, *Dignitatis Humanae*, is probably the most important.

However important these sixteen documents are, if they simply occupy space on library shelves, their purpose is defeated. We are just beginning to realize how rich these documents are in the living Tradition of the Church and how vital they are to the ongoing *magisterium* of the Church.

After almost every ecumenical council there has been a period of pause, while both the Fathers of the Council and the People of God sit back to see just what has been accomplished.

There are always a few ultraconservatives who claim that "they" went too far. Usually they are balanced out by another few who claim that "they" didn't go far enough. True to form, we saw that happen after Vatican II.

But with the passage of time, the "reform and renewal" of Vatican II has taken firm hold from the parish and individual level on up. What St. Charles Borromeo, St. Turibio Mongrovejo, St. Robert Bellarmine and others had to do after the Council of Trent has been embraced by a vast number of contemporary bishops who are determined to make Vatican II a pastoral reality.

Mary, Mother of the Church, will be our firm patroness as we do all we can to build up the Body of Christ, which is His Church. As she nourished Him in the small home at Nazareth, as she stood by Him on Calvary, she is very interested and involved in nourishing the Church in our lifetimes and seeing it through the rites of passage into the twenty-first century.

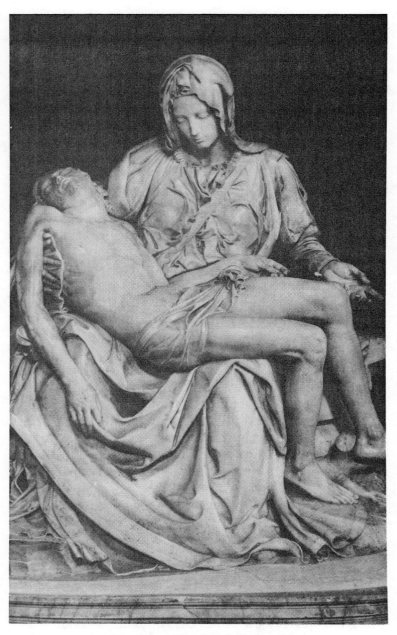

"La Pieta" by Michelangelo

17

Virgin Most Prudent
(Virgin Most Wise)

"In his will is our peace!" Dante considered the human condition and our striving for happiness, and instead of seeing just the human pursuits, he looked for the eternal purpose, since the Incarnation has changed human history. And where can man look for perfect happiness? What goals must he attain? Dante replied with tremendous wisdom: "In his will is our peace!"

In this title we salute Mary, the prudent virgin, the one with the practical wisdom to guide her life toward God. St. Alphonsus Liguori was so convinced of the fruits of the Immaculate Conception in the soul of Mary, that he tells us from the first moment of her conception by Joachim and Ann, she was completely in accord with the will of God.

She grew in this and all the practices of virtue by reason of her own natural growth and the maturing processes. This did not keep her from the experiences of her own childhood and adolescence, and her work in the Holy Family at Nazareth. She and St. Joseph constantly had to make decisions, sometimes guided by heavenly help, but more often by their own wisdom and prudence.

The question of her engagement to St. Joseph was the first example of her wisdom that we are aware of. That there had been others as she grew up cannot be doubted.

St. Therese of Lisieux tells us that from the age of three she never refused God anything. St. Stanislaus Kostka, the heroic boy, fought constantly to keep himself from worldly pursuits. St. Aloysius, who died as a young Jesuit long before he was old enough for ordination, says that he turned totally to God at the age of seven. The tales are almost endless about saints and their devotion to God that began at a young age.

Certainly, we can expect that this was true of Our Lady. The story of her Presentation in the Temple at the age of three does not rest on good historical evidence, but it has been greeted with delight by the Christian imagination of artists and poets. In extending the feast to the universal Church, the Church expects us to see in this possible event an example of total dedication and spirituality.

With the question of the marriage of Joseph and Mary, we have the undoubted question of Mary's virginity. If she didn't take a vow, as such, she had certainly dedicated herself to God as a virgin, as is evident from her reply to the Archangel Gabriel.

The Jewish faith is very familiar with vows, such as the vow of celibacy St. Paul took, so it is not unlikely that Mary was actually vowed to virginity. The opinion of the learned authors is that St. Joseph was also confirmed in virtue and probably had also vowed to virginity.

So it was a matter of prudent judgment between the two of them to seek the legal protection that Mary could have only in marriage, as well as the mutual love and support that transcended any passionate love.

The prudence of St. Joseph in the face of Mary's pregnancy is another example, one that could only be resolved by the angelic message. That one was beyond human prudence.

Then there was the matter of the journey to Bethlehem. Certainly conventional wisdom would have dictated that a pregnant woman should have stayed home and been exempt from the imperial decree.

Yet, in a small town such as Nazareth, the number of months of the marriage of Mary and Joseph, and the nine months for the birth of Jesus, would have left all the gossips with too much to say.

To save Mary's reputation it was the prudent thing to leave for Bethlehem and stay there until the time for the Egyptian exile. When they finally returned to Nazareth there would be no scandal. This also fulfilled two prophecies that Christ would be born in Bethlehem and that He would be called out of Egypt.

How did Mary and Joseph finance the flight into Egypt? It has been suggested that the gifts brought by the Magi were sold and the proceeds used to support the move into alien territory. More than likely the Holy Family lived in a Jewish community in one of the larger cities, where the language would not have been a difficulty.

At Nazareth, Mary would have to be a part of the small community and no doubt she was often asked for advice. We can legitimately wonder if Christ worked unobtrusive miracles there, because Mary had no difficulty in suggesting the miracle of the water turned to wine at Cana of Galilee.

Note that Our Lord seemed more to question the timing and the publicity of the miracle, not her request for it. And He worked the miracle!

We could go on through the Public Life and consider the position of Mary, since we know that she was among the holy women who followed Him. They were sort of a support staff, an incipient religious community.

At the Crucifixion, the Apostles did not think it at all prudent to be present. Mary, however, stood at the foot of the Cross, offering her Son with Him.

It is piously believed, as recorded by Francis Suarez, that Mary enjoyed the presence of Jesus throughout the forty days between the Resurrection and the Ascension. And we can only try to imagine what graces filled her, who was already full of grace, at Pentecost. During the remainder of her earthly life she must have been called upon often to use her wisdom and experience for the benefit of the infant Church.

Many think that St. Luke's first two chapters come directly from the memory of the Blessed Mother, since he reveals things that only she would have known with such eyewitness detail.

At the end of her life, she must have been filled with that desire of which St. Augustine writes, "the desire and longing for the courts of the Living God" which is common to all the saints. "O God, you have made us for yourself, and our hearts are restless until they rest in you."

This is the wisdom we salute in Mary, the Virgin most prudent. We ask her help in all the decisions we have to make to be true to the duties of our state in life. We live in a world which makes many complex demands on us. Our teenagers are faced with pressures and conflicts we never imagined when we were that age.

In the words of the most ancient Marian prayer, first found in a Greek papyrus dated about A.D. 300, we pray:

We turn to you for protection,
holy Mother of God.
Listen to our prayers
and help us in our needs.
Save us from every danger,
glorious and blessed Virgin. *Sub tuum praesidium*

18

Virgin Most Venerable
(Virgin Rightly Praised)

When Blessed Junipero Serra was declared "Venerable" by the Holy Father, most Catholics in California were overjoyed at this honor. He was a humble Franciscan Friar with a good education and a high sense of his mission.

As a matter of fact, he had become an experienced missionary during his years of work in Mexico and he came to the California Missions with a great deal of mission expertise. He dedicated the rest of his life to the Indians and to building up the Church in this vast new land.

He was strict with his converts, considering them the "children of the human race," and their rebirth in Christ he considered his paternal responsibility. He took it very seriously.

So, the title "Venerable" suits him perfectly. Now that he has been beatified, we hope that he will make rapid progress toward canonization.

But is this the sense in which we call Mary "venerable"? Yes, and more so. The dictionary defines venerable as worthy of reverence or respect by virtue of dignity, character, position or age.

While we never think of the Blessed Mother as old, her dignity, character and position have no equal on earth, nor will they ever. Chosen by the Father to be the mother of His Son, prepared by the Holy Spirit to be worthy of her vocation, and saluted by the angel as "Full of grace," she comes with the highest seal of approval that heaven can give.

God has honored her first and foremost, and the Church imitates Him in singing her praises. The form of veneration given to the saints in general is called *dulia* by the theologians. However, the honor given to Mary is referred to as *hyperdulia* and to St. Joseph as *protodulia* because of their closeness to Christ.

The Fathers and Doctors of the Church have been the voice of that praise both in the East and in the West. There is an absolutely remarkable unanimity in their works on Mariology.

St. Justin Martyr, in the mid-second century of the Christian era, starts off the chorus of praise: "Isaiah foretold, 'Behold a virgin shall conceive and bear a Son and his name shall be called Emmanuel' (i.e., God with us). For what man has deemed incredible and impossible, God foretold through the prophetic spirit.

"The words mean that the virgin shall conceive without intercourse. For if she had had intercourse with anyone whomsoever, she was no longer a virgin, but the power of God descending upon the virgin overshadowed her and caused her, while still a virgin, to conceive."

St. Irenaeus, later in that same century, in defending the young Church against its first heretics, writes, "The seduction of a fallen angel drew Eve a virgin soon to be united with her husband, while the glad tidings of the holy angel drew Mary, a virgin already espoused, to begin the plan which would dissolve the bonds of the first snare. . . .

"The Virgin Mary has become the advocate for the virgin Eve. Death was brought upon the world by a virgin; life has triumphed by the Virgin Mary's obedience, which has finally balanced the debt of disobedience."

In commenting on the Gospel of St. Luke, St. Ambrose proclaims, "See the humility! Note well the devotion. She who has been chosen to be the Mother of the Lord calls herself his little servant girl. She certainly does not become haughty over this promise of so exalted a position. By calling herself a handmaiden she does not take as a right what is freely given as a grace."

The great biblical scholar, St. Jerome, is just as fervent: "When the angel cried 'Hail, full of grace, the Lord is with you; you are blessed among women!' he told us by divine command how tremendous was the dignity and beauty of the ever-virgin Mary.

"How well we can understand that she would be 'full of grace,' this Virgin who glorified God and gave our Lord to mankind, who poured out peace upon the earth by giving hope to the gentiles, protection against temptation, purpose of life and reason for sacrifice."

Down through the centuries, each age has competed in showing how much the men and women of their times venerated the Blessed Mother. And in these, our times, eloquent voices have been raised to join us to this chorus.

Archbishop Fulton Sheen was the voice of the American Church in the pre-Vatican II times. He writes, "In the streets of the Roman world, of which Israel was but a conquered part, there stands an exultant woman proclaiming to all the world the tidings of her emancipation. 'He that is Mighty has done great things for me.' It was a representative voice, not only of Israel, but of womanhood and the world. It was the clarion call of a long-repressed sex claiming its right and hailing its emancipation. . . .

"Not in her times alone, but in her for all times, woman would find her glory and her honor. They could not call her Jew nor Greek nor Roman; not successful nor beautiful, but 'blessed,' that is, holy. And blessed she is because by giving birth to the God-Man she broke down the trammels of nationality and race. He is MAN *par excellence*. And she is THE WOMAN because she is the Mother of God."

Perhaps even more eloquent is this excerpt from Dorothy Day's journal, "On Pilgrimage," for March 8, 1948: "So I am trying to recall my soul like the straying creature it is as it wanders off over and over again during the day, and lift my heart to the Blessed Mother and the saints, since my occupations are the lowly and humble ones, as were theirs."

Pope John Paul II, in proclaiming the Second Marian Year, 1987-88, in his encyclical *Redemptoris Mater*, wanted to emphasize the special bond between humanity and the Mother of God. He recalled the teaching of the Second Vatican Council, in *Lumen Gentium* (No. 66 and No. 67), which spoke not only of the doctrines of faith but the life of faith, and the place that Marian spirituality has in enlivening them.

He concludes, "Mary belongs indissolubly to the mystery of Christ, and she belongs also to the mystery of the Church from the beginning, from the day of the Church's birth."

Venerable, indeed, is this Virgin, so rightly, so justly praised by the whole Church.

19

Virgin Most Renowned
(Virgin Rightly Renowned)

The praises of the Blessed Virgin Mary are preached throughout the Catholic world with great joy. Her renown is on the lips of the learned and the scholarly, as well as the ordinary, devout Catholic.

It would be impossible to number the cathedrals, basilicas, churches, schools and institutions that have been erected to the glory of God under her patronage. It's hard to imagine a Catholic church that does not have a Marian altar, statue or picture.

She has been preached about by all the Fathers and Doctors of the Church, even though the vast majority of their works tended to be strictly theological. St. Bernard and St. Alphonsus Liguori, whose names are synonymous with love for Mary, devoted only a tiny part of their writings to Mariology — but how eloquent they are on the subject!

Individual titles for Mary are also impossible to number, although she is honored somewhere in the world on every day of the year with one or more festal titles.

When the custom of linking Mary to local territories started, the combinations were limitless. Consider Our Lady of the Genesee, Our Lady of New Melleray, Our Lady of Pompeii and we can come all the way down to Our Lady of Poway!

What is of special interest to many Catholics are the many places of pilgrimage that draw us like magnets.

One of the most venerable and visited shrines in the New World is that of Our Lady of Guadalupe in Mexico City. Who can even dream of the number of miracles, spiritual and physical healings, and answered prayers attributed to Mary at that shrine?

We are told that in 1531 Mary appeared four times to a young Indian named Juan Diego, on Tepeyac hill, which was then outside of Mexico City. She directed him to go to Bishop Juan Zumarraga, the first Bishop of Mexico City, one of the "Twelve Apostles of Mexico," and ask that a church be built in her honor on the spot where she appeared.

The bishop, of course, demanded proof. He was finally convinced when he saw the life-sized picture of Mary that she had painted on the Indian's simple cloak, or mantle. Shortly after, a little chapel was built on the spot.

It has been rebuilt several times and now is a very modern and beautiful basilica. In 1945, Pope Pius XII designated Our Lady of Guadalupe as the patroness of the Americas. The motto chosen for the shrine is "God has not done thus for any other nation" (Ps 147:20).

Two other shrines in North America that are close to the hearts of Mary's followers are the Shrine to St. Joseph in Montreal and the Shrine of St. Anne-de-Beaupre in rural Quebec. It is a thrill to witness and participate in the candle-light procession at this latter shrine on almost every night in the summer.

In speaking of Marian shrines, certainly the most famous in the world would be Our Lady of Lourdes. In 1858 Mary appeared 18 times to St. Bernardette Soubirous in the grotto of Massabielle, which was near Lourdes in southern France. She identified herself as the Immaculate Conception to the fourteen-year-old girl.

The local clergy and bishop were not pleased with the stories told by Bernardette. It was only after four years of rigorous examination that the local bishop allowed a chapel to be built there as requested by Mary.

As at Guadalupe, the reputation for healings and miracles is preached throughout the land, and pilgrims arrive in droves. An old English saying tells us that the saint who grants few favors has few pilgrims. The witness of the Catholic world to the effectiveness of Mary's intercession at Lourdes is well known everywhere.

Pope Leo XIII authorized the local feast of Our Lady of Lourdes for February 11, and Pope St. Pius X extended the feast to the whole world in 1907. The underground Church of St. Pius X at Lourdes is reputedly the second largest Christian Church in the world, holding 20,000 persons.

At Fatima in Portugal, Mary appeared six times to three children in a field called Cova de Iria, north of Lisbon. Only after seven years of canonical investigations were the 1917 apparitions declared worthy of belief. Devotion here centered around the Rosary and the Immaculate Heart of Mary.

In 1942 Pope Pius XII consecrated the world to the Immaculate Heart of Mary, and ten years later he specifically consecrated the people of Russia to her as she had requested at Fatima. Continuing prayers for world peace and the conversion of Russia are an integral part of the Fatima devotion.

The medal of the Immaculate Conception, known affectionately as the Miraculous Medal, was commissioned by Mary in three apparitions to St. Catherine Laboure at Paris, in 1830. She was, at the time, in the chapel of the Motherhouse of the Daughters of Charity of St. Vincent de Paul.

Lesser known, but still very popular shrines are at LaSalette in France, and at Banneux and Beauraing in Belgium. Devotions to Our Lady of LaSalette have been confirmed by popes since Pius IX. The Belgian shrines have the approval of the local ordinaries.

One thing in common with most Marian apparitions is the Christ-centered nature of what Mary asks. She encourages upright Christian living, concern for the conversion of sinners and promotion of the prayer life of her children. Her devotees are always encouraged to use the sacraments fruitfully. The Scapular of Our Lady of Mount Carmel is also one of the widely known Marian devotions. The scapular originally was an apron that was thrown over the religious habit, reaching down from the shoulders both in front and in back.

According to a pious legend in the Carmelite Order, Our Lady is said to have appeared to St. Simon Stock and promised that anyone who died while wearing the Carmelite scapular would surely be saved, and if they had to go to Purgatory, Mary would come and lead them to heaven on the first Saturday following their death.

This claim has never been subjected to serious investigation, and since it comes from the thirteenth century, that investigation would now be decidedly late. However it does testify to the fact of Mary's powerful intercession and the use of sacramentals to help daily Christian living.

The Scapular Medal, approved by Pope St. Pius X in 1910, and the Miraculous Medal, are two of the most popular medals worn by Catholics. It is possible to obtain one medal with both images.

Even as this is being written, apparitions of the Blessed Mother are being reported in Yugoslavia in the little town of Medjugorje. Six young people have claimed to see her frequently from June 24, 1981 until this present day. While the bishop of that diocese has not yet given this devotion his approval, the Marian message seems consistent with real devotion to her.

Briefly stated, the Medjugorje message has five main points: 1. commitment to God, including monthly Confession; 2. faith, including frequent recital of the Apostles Creed; 3. prayer, with emphasis on the Mass, Communion, the Rosary and mental prayer; 4. fasting, from the bread-and-water type to lesser abstentions; 5. praying and working for world peace. She asks that June 25 be set aside each year to honor her as Queen of Peace.

All of these pious practices demonstrate the reputation that Mary has for her powerful patronage. Hers is the honor, the renown, rightly shown by devout children, just as we sing in the popular hymn, "Yours are the praises unclaimed by another."

20
Virgin Most Powerful

Spiritual power, spiritual strength consists of holiness, the triumph of the grace of Christ in our souls. No one can compare with Mary for her heights of holiness. As we have seen, the saints tell us that all the holiness in the rest of creation combined does not equal that which enhanced the soul of the Blessed Virgin.

In the *Magnificat* the Holy Spirit has Mary cry out, "He who is mighty has done great things in me — *Fecit mihi magna qui potens est*" (Lk 1:49). This holiness was given to Mary at the instant of her conception, and it continued to grow through her contact with Christ, especially during the Hidden Years at Nazareth.

When Christ wanted to teach us how to pray, and how to grow in closer union with God, He taught His disciples the Lord's Prayer. In the petitions of the Our Father, we have a capsule or digest version of the blueprints for holiness.

How Mary must have reveled in these thoughts while she had the time alone with Christ and listened to His ideas. As the handmaiden of the Father, how she must have longed to make His name holy among all peoples.

"Hallowed be your Name" was a driving force for St. Ignatius Loyola. As he lay in that Spanish castle recuperating and contemplating the Faith in Northern Europe devastated by Luther's rebellion, the thought of proclaiming the Lord's name urged him on in his resolve to form the Society of Jesus.

At that same time, the Holy Spirit was raising up other champions for the Counter-reformation — Teresa a child at Avila, Xavier a university student, Peter Faber a schoolboy, etc. And if this love for God's holy name inspired these people, consider how it must have played in the soul of Mary! "The Kingdom of God" was a major theme in the public preaching of Jesus Christ. That Mary was to reign as the queen in that Kingdom forever was only a part of the dignity that attached her office as Mother of God.

"Your will be done" was a major factor in the Incarnation, for it was in obedience to His Father's will that Christ became man and, as He conspicuously proved during the agony on the garden of Gethsemane, it was devotion to and obedience to that will that sustained Him throughout His Passion and death.

The early Church was amazed at this quality of obedience in Christ. Certainly this was a virtue He learned and practiced at Nazareth, when He returned there and was subject to Mary and Joseph.

Dante, in speaking of the will of God, says quite simply, "In his Will is our peace."

So powerful is Mary's role in the whole economy of salvation that the Church proclaims in her offices, "Rejoice, O Virgin Mary, for you alone have destroyed all the heresies in the whole world!"

When the Council of Ephesus solemnly defined Mary's position as "Mother of God," it saved and defended the fundamental doctrine of the Incarnation, that Jesus is true God and true man. All heresies ultimately revolve around that truth, and Mary, the Mother, has triumphed over all of them.

This powerful virgin Mother is praised by the Church through the use of three very powerful feminine figures in the Bible. The Woman who will crush the head of the serpent through her Son, in Genesis; the Woman who commands a public miracle at Cana of Galilee, and the Woman of the Apocalypse, Revelations, whose Son is to save the world, are the figures of Mary's power with Christ.

Mary as the type of Eve, indeed the New Eve to Our Lord's position as the New Adam, was much admired by the Fathers and Doctors of the Church.

St. Bernard has Adam and Eve exult in Mary's vocation. "Rejoice, O Father Adam, and even more, rejoice and exult, Mother Eve. You, the first parents of all the living, have unfortunately given life to mankind tainted with sin. But now you can be comforted in your great daughter. O Eve, the shame that you have passed down to all women will now be taken away."

In another place he writes, "Eve was a thorn but Mary was a rose. Eve, the thorn, inflicted wounds, but Mary, the rose, soothed all passions. Eve, the thorn, brought death, but Mary, the rose, made salvation accessible."

And in a sermon on the Apocalypse, Bernard repeats the theme. "That most prudent Sculptor did not break up what had been crushed, but he refashioned it in a yet better way. From human flesh he formed a New Adam, and in Mary, he uncovered a New Eve.

"Know, O man, the plan of God. Recognize the plan of his wisdom, the counsel of his love. The price of universal salvation has been given us through Mary, that she might retrieve the reputation of our first mother, Eve.

"From Eve came that most cruel poison, sin. Through Mary, God has bestowed on us a most merciful antidote. Eve brought seduction; Mary brings propitiation. Eve brought deceit; Mary brings Truth."

St. Irenaeus reminds us that "Eve listened and lost God; Mary listened and obeyed God. The Virgin Mary has become the advocate for the virgin Eve. Death was brought into the world by a virgin; life has triumphed by the Virgin. Mary's obedience has finally balanced the debt of disobedience."

St. Augustine returns to this theme several times, namely that "Eve mourned, but Mary exulted. Eve carried tears in her womb; Mary carried joy. . . . From Eve came sin; from Mary, grace. . . . The miraculous new birth has conquered the cause of grief. Mary's song of praise quiets the mourning of Eve."

The final chapter of the Book of Proverbs contains the tribute to the ideal wife as understood in the Jewish Law (Prv 31:10-31). The Church frequently applies these verses to Mary, as the Valiant Woman beyond compare.

The picture of a strong woman who understood her own vocation, who exercises prudence and charity, who turns a house into a loving, warm home, is still a delight, and Mary certainly knew this ideal and practiced it. She was undoubtedly the delight of her husband, St. Joseph.

The question, academic as it is, has been raised, "Did Mary work any miracles in her own lifetime on earth?" The saints are inclined to a positive answer to this question.

Whether she did or not, she deserves the title Virgin Most Powerful for the shower of miracles she has obtained from God throughout the Christian centuries. As practical modern men and women, we will continue to beg her intercession, and expect results!

21

Virgin Most Merciful
(Virgin Gentle in Mercy)

"Hail, holy Queen, Mother of mercy. . . ." begins a prayer that we recite with almost every Rosary and at many other times. St. Alphonsus Liguori wrote his famous treatise, *The Glories of Mary*, primarily as a commentary on this prayer.

That she is a Queen, he affirms, is beyond question, since her Son is King of all creation. The importance of the King's mother is evident in the history of the kingdoms of Israel and Judah, and the post of Queen Mother had real power in the age when Alphonsus lived.

Since Mary is the Mother of the Head of the Church, she is also the Mother of the members of the body. On Calvary, when Christ gave Mary to St. John and St. John to Mary, the saints see the symbolic bestowal of the whole human race into her maternal care.

St. Bernardine of Siena writes, "By these words, Mary, by reason of the love she bore them, became the Mother, not only of St. John, but of all mankind."

Mary, then, assumes an important role in the history of mankind as Queen and Mother. And just as Christ redeemed us in His great mercy and love, so He joins Mary to Himself in this work.

Sin deprives our souls of the grace of Christ and so robs our soul of life. Jesus "so loved the world that he gave his life for our salvation," and as He tells us, "I have come that you may have life and have it more abundantly" (Jn 10:10).

In the divine plan for our salvation, Mary gave us Jesus and Jesus gave us the real life of grace. To call Mary the Virgin-Mother Most Merciful is simply to see a reflection in her of the mercy that Christ dispensed to the world. St. Albert the Great states it quite simply when he says that by consenting to conceive Christ in her womb she became our spiritual Mother.

She also became our spiritual Mother when she cooperated with Christ in His offering on Calvary. As St. Augustine says, by doing this, "she then cooperated by her love in the birth of the faithful to the life of grace and became the spiritual Mother of all who are members of the one head, Christ Jesus."

The Church frequently applies these words to Mary: "I am the mother of fair love" (Eccl 24:24). To this St. Bonaventure comments, "And what mother loves her children and attends to their welfare as you do, O most sweet Queen? You love us and seek our care far more than any earthly mother."

St. Robert Bellarmine adds, "Nor will this most loving Virgin hesitate to embrace in her maternal love so great a multitude of children. She ardently desires that not a single soul perish whom her Son has redeemed by his own precious Blood in his saving death."

St. Bonaventure comments: "The grace of God, so necessary to heal mankind, is dispensed to us through her. As from an aqueduct, grace flows through Mary. What her Son won by strict right, Mary dispenses as a most merciful Queen, having compassion on her needy people."

"When the storms of temptation rage, the most compassionate Mother of the faithful, with maternal tenderness, protects them as it were in her own bosom until she has brought them into the harbor of salvation." St. Alphonsus adopts these words from the writer Novarinus.

Our lady herself once assured St. Bridget of Sweden, "As a mother on seeing her son in the midst of the swords of his enemies, would use every effort to save him, so do I, and will do it for all sinners who seek my mercy." "O happy confidence!" exclaims St. Anselm, "O safe refuge! the Mother of God is my Mother. How firm then, should be our confidence, since our salvation depends on the judgment of a good Brother and a tender Mother."

Mary learned mercy from Jesus, the Holy Redeemer, the Good Shepherd, the Sacred Heart and from all the other tender aspects of His love. She learned how great the price of mercy is when she stood at the foot of the cross. She did not flinch or draw back, for she found her strength in Him, and for rest of eternity she will share that mercy with all her children, all of us.

Think of what this Christian love and mercy have inspired in the lives of the saints and the countless holy men and women through the Christian dispensation.

Martyrs shed their blood in abundance to nourish the infant Church, and martyrs continued to do so in every age. We do not have to look back just on the Coliseum to see that the blood of martyrs is the seed of Christians.

The Church in the present day United States and Canada can look back on the pioneer missionaries who often lost their lives in the service of the "noble savages." St. John Brebeuf, St. Isaac Jogues and their Companions, the priests and brothers in Georgia, Father Luis Jayme in California, Father Pro in Mexico City and many others gave of themselves for love of God and neighbor.

We remember Bishop Oscar Romero and priests and nuns in modern times who have given their lives in Central America.

But if this is true of the saints, it is even more so of the Blessed Mother. Her martyrdom was complete on Calvary, and so far superior to all the others that she can dispense the mercy of God as a proven emissary of God.

"Because all men have been redeemed by Jesus,"

writes St. Alphonsus, "therefore Mary loves and protects them all. It was she who was seen by St. John in the Apocalypse, clothed with the sun. As no one can hide from the heat of the sun, so no one can hide from the love and mercy of Jesus. So, also, no one can be deprived of the love of Mary."

Mary once told St. Bridget that she was the mother not only of the just and innocent, but also of sinners, provided they were willing to repent. How promptly, then, does a sinner who is desirous of amendment and entrusts himself to her intercession, find that this good Mother will embrace and help him.

St. Gregory VII wrote in this way to the princess Matilda, "Resolve to sin no more and I promise that undoubtedly you will find Mary more ready to love you than any earthly mother."

St. Peter Nolasco founded the Order of Our Lady of Mercy, or of Ransom, to provide relief for slaves and captives taken by the Mohammedans, early in the thirteenth century. He was encouraged to do this by the Blessed Mother in a private revelation.

Our Lady was interested in the redemption of slaves who were abused by their masters and deprived of their liberty. She pities even more those who are slaves to sin and we turn to her to lead us to the mercy of God. St.

Bernard remarks, "Let him cease to praise your mercy who remembers having ever invoked you without being graciously heard." Mary is as clement and as merciful toward those who have recourse to her as she is powerful with God.

St. Alphonsus prays, "O most loving Mother! O most compassionate Mother! May you ever be blessed, and ever blessed be God who has given you to us for our Mother, and for a secure Refuge in all the dangers of this life."

22

Virgin Most Faithful
(Faithful Virgin)

St. Paul uses the word "faith" 146 times in his Epistles, and words like faithful, faithfully and faithless occur almost as often. In his struggle against the Judaizers, he had to prove that salvation came from faith in Christ, a grace dearly won and freely given, and not from the works of the Law.

In 1 Corinthians 13 he shows his converts that this must be a living faith, one that comes alive through charity. "If I speak with the tongues of men and angels. ... If I have faith so that I can move mountains. ... but have not charity. ... I am nothing, a tinkling cymbal, a noisy gong. ..."

All of this we see summed up in the life of the Blessed Virgin. She was the First Christian, the first to believe in Jesus Christ, the Son of God, the Savior.

God chose to need Mary for the Incarnation. He sent the Archangel Gabriel to ask Mary's *consent* before the Incarnation happened. At her *fiat*, the almighty Word of God came down from Heaven to take His place in her womb.

Mary's faith continued to grow throughout her lifetime. When she went to visit St. Elizabeth who was pregnant with St. John the Baptizer, these two prophetesses had three months to ponder over all that had been said about the Savior in the Old Testament.

The prophet Isaiah, especially, always a favorite with the early Church Fathers, must have been the subject of great conversations between these two women. He had foretold that a virgin would conceive and bear a son, and that the child would be called *Emmanuel*, God-with-us. This was certainly fulfilled in a way more literal than anyone could have expected.

Then St. Joseph had to be told and Mary's faith was tested as he pondered what he was to do, until the same Archangel took Joseph's doubts and fears away. Mary, so far superior to Joseph in sanctity, still subjected herself to him as was expected of an upright Jewish wife, and expected that the directions to save the Child Jesus would come to her through her husband.

Throughout the Hidden Years, Mary and Joseph had to nourish, protect and cherish the growing Lad. He had to be trained as a carpenter, or more probably, a day laborer. When Our Lord used stories about the workers gathering in the marketplace waiting to be hired, it is likely it was something he had experienced.

All the while, as the Child grew, so did Mary's faith and love, being exercised in so close a personal, family way. She kept all these things carefully in her heart. She treasured them in her memory and exulted in them.

Were there quiet, unobtrusive miracles around the little hamlet of Nazareth? I think so. There would have been so many demands for good works to help sincere and faithful neighbors. Mary certainly expected a miracle at Cana without any preliminaries that we can ascertain.

Throughout His Public Life, Mary was never far from Him. How her soul grew as she listened to Him teach the multitudes and witnessed His miracles. How many times she must have smiled to herself when she heard the Apostles ponder over the words of wisdom He shared directly with them. No doubt she had heard all of this in the home at Nazareth.

When a woman from the crowd cried, "Blessed is the womb that bore you and the breasts that nursed you," Jesus immediately turned it into praise of His Mother, "Rather, blessed are they who hear the word of God and keep it" (Lk 11:27-28). Mary was the outstanding example of that. And when Christ walked the *Via Dolorosa*, Mary's faith and love made her follow Him, step by step. The saints assure us that her faith never faltered, but it grew and helped her share His offering of Himself to the Father.

St. Ambrose tells us, "His Mother stood by the Cross. Impervious to the crowd, she stands firm. Despite her natural modesty, the brave soul of the Mother of Jesus endures the public scorn.

"Her eyes take in those precious wounds which she knows are the price of redemption for all mankind. She did not back off from this terrible sight, any more than she drew off from the terrible executioners."

And further on, "The other evangelists tell us about the earthquake when Christ died, the threatening skies, the darkened sun, the thief's heavenly reward after his holy confession of faith.

"John fills in the things the others passed over, especially that he called Mary 'Mother' from the Cross. John obviously feels that when Christ, the conqueror of death, gives the example of filial love, it is more important than the bestowal of Paradise on a dying thief. If it is an awe-inspiring act to show mercy at such a time, it is yet more wonderful for the Son of God to show such honor to his Mother."

On that first Holy Saturday, when the Apostles and disciples must have been shocked to their very foundations, when their fear of the Jewish and Roman officials drove them underground, Mary must have pondered the prophecies of Isaiah and Jeremiah which saw Christ as the Suffering Servant of Yahweh. "He was despised and rejected by men, a man of sorrows. . ." (Is 53:3-5).

And then the joy, the triumph of Easter! It is the considered opinion of many of the writers that Mary enjoyed Christ's presence throughout the forty days when He appeared in His Risen Body. That Body which was able to penetrate locked doors, was also able to bilocate.

As soon as He rose from the dead, He appeared to Mary and continued on with her until the Ascension.

How much longer Mary stayed on earth before her own triumphant Assumption into Heaven is not known. It seems that she had a part to play in the spread of the Church of Christ. It is also the traditional opinion that she gave St. Luke the material for the first two chapters of his Gospel, as well as many other details. This still seems very logical.

In his encyclical *Mother of the Redeemer*, Part 1, Section 2, Pope John Paul II teaches lovingly of the faith of Mary: "Through this faith, Mary is perfectly united with Christ in his self-emptying. For Christ Jesus, who, though he was in the form of God, did not count equality with God a thing to be grasped, but emptied himself, taking the form of a servant, being born in the likeness of men: precisely on Golgotha, humbled himself and became obedient until death, even death on a cross (cf. Phil 2:5-8).

"At the foot of the cross Mary shares through faith in the shocking mystery of this self-emptying. This is perhaps the deepest kenosis of faith in human history. Through faith the Mother shares in the death of her Son, in his redeeming death; but in contrast with the faith of the disciples who fled, hers was far more enlightened. . . . In the expression 'Blessed is she who believed,' we can therefore rightly find a kind of key which unlocks for us the innermost reality of Mary, whom the angel hailed as 'full of grace.' If as 'full of grace' she has been eternally present in the mystery of Christ, through faith she became a sharer in that mystery in every extension of her earthly journey. She 'advanced in her pilgrimage of faith' and at the same time, in a discreet yet direct and effective way, she made present to humanity the mystery of Christ. And she still continues to do so."

O faithful Virgin, guide us along the paths of faith to grow to full maturity in Christ!

23
Mirror of Justice

In the seminary, we were subjected to a very intense course in the social encyclicals, starting with Pope Leo XIII's *Rerum Novarum*. As a matter of fact, it was a very practical and useful course, one that came in very handy during the civil-rights years that followed World War II.

The rights of working men and their employers, the social dimension of the hungry, the homeless and the refugee, the crime of discrimination on the basis of race, religion or sex and a host of other problems came under study in this course on "Justice."

But when we turn to theology, the term has an even more important dimension. It covers the entire notion of holiness, of righteousness, of justification. We are holy, right and just in the sight of God insofar as Christ is formed in us.

When we apply the title "Mirror of Justice" to Our Lady, we have the most perfect image of God that can be found in a mere human soul. Starting with the tremendous privilege of her Immaculate Conception, there is no stain or blemish that can mar the Godlike image in her soul.

When St. Paul spoke of the image of God, he knew the ancient mirrors of pounded metal, which gave a very imperfect image, and that was all he had to go on. "At present we see indistinctly, as in a mirror, but then face to face" (1 Cor 13:12).

In Mary, the mirror reflects back exactly what it images. As the prophet Malachi spoke of Christ as "the sun of justice with its healing rays" (Mal 3:20) so the Son, reflected in Mary's soul, is a perfect image.

It is no wonder that the saints referred so often to Mary as the moon reflecting the sun's brilliance. According to St. Alphonsus, "She can only reflect back what is mirrored from her Son. And it is always as perfect an image as a creature can reflect."

At one time, I believe, the observatory at Palomar Mountain in Southern California had the largest reflecting mirror in the world in its telescope. I well remember that it was front-page news, with details on how it was polished, assembled and used. Now there have been even more advances since then, with radio telescopes and orbiting telescopes.

The scientists spare no expense to get as clear an image of the universe as is humanly possible. How that pales into insignificance in the eternal beauty reflected in Mary's soul!

Mankind, we are told, is made in the image and likeness of God. At least three times the Book of Genesis makes that point. As we well know, it is not that God has a head, arms, legs, etc. We are like God in His spirit, in the immortal soul that He has given us.

We image God because we have intellects that search for truth, and free wills that can seek love. In these most vital things we are created in the image and likeness of God. When we consider Mary's dignity, we can only begin to imagine how much she mirrors the God of Love, the God of Truth.

It is enough to make the whole heavenly court draw back in wonder at what God has wrought in the woman "full of grace." The angels, we are told, veil their faces before God, yet Mary can reflect the image of God in a soul made perfect by the actions of the Holy Spirit in her.

There is another interesting thought about the human reflection between Jesus and Mary. Since no male seed went into His conception, He took all of His human characteristics from His Blessed Mother. He had to look exactly like her, saving only for the difference of sex.

How often we have seen old married couples who seem to take on each other's characteristics, even as to looks. But with Jesus and Mary, we have to have a biological exact replica in facial matters.

Obviously, it is more important that she mirror Him in the quality of the soul and the spiritual life, but it is an interesting speculation about their human characteristics.

Adam and Eve resembled God as they came forth from creation. Their souls did not know sin. Only when they, in pride, sought to become "like gods" did they mar the terrible beauty of their pristine souls. When Christ, the New Adam brought redemption to the children of Adam and Eve, Mary, the New Eve brought humanity to its fullest reflection of the image of God possible in a human soul.

It is also interesting to note that when Mary has appeared at various shrines, the impression of her beauty is outstanding. St. Bernardette tried to explain and describe her, and could only repeat over and over again, "So beautiful, so young and beautiful, such as I have never ever seen."

The three children at Fatima had the same trouble when an artist was commissioned to make an official portrait of Our Lady of Fatima. They described her over and over again, to no avail.

She looked like the statue of her in their parish church, or else how would they have recognized her? But her beauty was so far beyond that, that they gave up trying to correct the painter's work.

When you stand at the altar in the Shrine of Our Lady of Guadalupe in Mexico City, you have to be impressed with the eyes in the image. They seem to follow you everywhere in the Church. I celebrated Mass at the main altar in the old shrine, and it was almost overpowering. There is a beauty to it that defies reproduction.

That exceeding beauty is a reflection of the beauty of God. He is the sun; she is the moon that gives a faithful reflection.

"Whoever sees God," Our Lady once remarked to St. Bridget of Sweden, "sees me; and whoever sees me may see the divinity and humanity in me as in a mirror and me in God. For whoever sees me, sees as it were, the Three Persons. For the Deity has enfolded me in itself with my soul and body, and filled me with every virtue, so that there is no virtue in God which does not shine forth in me."

Small wonder, then, that the Church applies these words on Wisdom to Mary: She "is the unspotted mirror of God's majesty, and the image of his goodness" (Wis 7:26).

Archbishop Fulton J. Sheen used to love this little verse, to reflect the interplay between Jesus and Mary, Son and Mother:

> Lovely Lady dressed in blue
> Teach me how to pray.
> God was just your little boy
> And you know the way.

24

Seat of Wisdom
(Throne of Wisdom)

There is an old aphorism that goes like this: *lex orandi, lex credendi,* which means, roughly, that the way we pray demonstrates what we believe. That makes the history of Catholic liturgy a real study in the unfolding of the official prayer life of the Church.

About the year 1000, when fear of the ending of the world swept across parts of Europe, the Church developed votive Masses as supplications for special needs. Naturally, a large number of Marian votive Masses were created.

In searching for biblical texts, the heart of a Liturgy of the Word, the usual verses were taken from the first part of St. Matthew and St. Luke, and also the passages that mention Mary in Christ's Public Life and His paschal mysteries. The Old Testament verses most used were taken from the Wisdom literature. These were used in an applied sense, of course, but they were used very generously.

Proverbs 8 was a particular delight in this development. Mary, as the personification of Wisdom speaks: "The Lord possessed me in the beginning of his ways, before he made anything, from the beginning. I was set up from eternity, and of old, before the earth was made.

"The depths were not as yet, and I was already conceived; neither had the fountains of waters as yet sprung out; the mountains with their huge bulk had not as yet been established; before the hills I was brought forth. He had not yet made the earth nor the rivers, nor the poles of the world.

"When he prepared the heavens, I was present; when with a certain law and compass he enclosed the depths; when he established the sky above, and poised the fountains of waters; when he compassed the sea with its bounds, and set a law to the waters that they should not pass their limits; when he balanced the foundations of the earth; I was with him forming all things; and was delighted every day, playing before him at all times; playing in the world; and my delights were to be with the children of men.

"Now, therefore, children, hear me: Blessed are they who keep my ways. Hear instruction and be wise, and refuse it not. Blessed is the man that hears me and that watches daily at my gates, and watches at my doorposts.

"He that shall find me shall find life and shall have salvation from the Lord" (Prv 8:22-35, Douay-Confraternity version).

It is not difficult to see the link between Wisdom and Mary. To start with, her unique relationship with the Holy Trinity: she is the Daughter of the Father, Spouse of the Holy Spirit, and Mother of the Son. Infinite Wisdom came into the world through her.

As every child reigns from the throne or seat of the mother's arms, so we would expect this title for Mary. St. Augustine seems to have been the first to use it, and St. Bernard used it and varieties of this theme several times.

About thirty years ago, a medieval text was discovered dating from around the end of the twelfth century, written by Abbot Odo of Battle Abbey. Father O'Carroll quotes from it in his book *Theotokos*:

"Philosophy is called the pursuit or love of wisdom. Mary is, therefore, the philosophy of Christians for whoever desire to find the true wisdom must direct all their love and endeavor towards Mary.

"But Christ who is called the power and wisdom of God, is the true Wisdom. He is strictly the true Wisdom of Christians for to another beyond him the Christian cannot go. Whoever desires to have this wisdom must direct his studies toward the Mother for in Mary must he study who is to find Christ.

"For through Mary we come to Christ as through a mother to a son; through the Mother of mercy to Mercy himself."

Cardinal John Henry Newman dedicated the Mary altar in the church he built in Dublin to Our Lady, Seat of Wisdom.

Newman wrote two beautiful sermons on the glories of Mary that are included in almost every collection of his works. He says that if we find it only right and just to honor all Mary's prerogatives, then, what must our response be?

"If the Mother of Emmanuel ought to be the first of creatures in sanctity and in beauty; if it becomes her to be free from all sin from the very first, and from the moment she received her first grace to begin to merit more; and if such was her beginning, such was her end, her conception immaculate and her death the assumption; if she died but revived and is exalted on high; what is befitting in the children of such a Mother, but an imitation, in their measure, of her devotion, her meekness, her simplicity, her modesty and her sweetness?

"Her glories are not only for the sake of her Son, they are for our sakes also. Let us copy her faith, who received God's message by the angel without a doubt; her patience, who endured St. Joseph's surprise without a word; her obedience, who went up to Bethlehem in the winter and bore the Lord in a stable; her meditative spirit, who pondered in her heart what she saw and heard about him; her fortitude, whose heart the sword went through; her self-surrender, who gave him up during his ministry and consented to his death."

Is it any wonder that she grew in experience and wisdom, in union with the Wisdom that became incarnate through her.

In my anthology of Abbot Columba Marmion's writing titled *Fire of Love*, the Benedictine abbot spends a chapter on the relationship of the Holy Spirit and Mary:

"Mary's faith was perfect, and, filled with the light of the Holy Spirit, her soul understood the value of the offering that she was making to God. By his inspirations, the Holy Spirit put her soul in harmony with the inward dispositions of the Heart of her divine Son.

"This intense faith which was a source of love for the Mother of God, was also a principle of joy. The Holy Spirit himself teaches us this, by the mouth of St. Elizabeth, when he declares that the Virgin is blessed forever because of her faith."

Further on he adds, "Imagine, then, with what predilection the Holy Trinity fashioned the immaculate heart of the Blessed Virgin, chosen to be the Mother of the Incarnate Word. God delighted in pouring forth love in her heart, in forming it expressly to love a God-Man."

Seminarians used to find in this title, Seat of Wisdom, a special attraction, since they were studying Christ, the source of Christian wisdom, and invoked Mary to help their learning. The story is told of St. Albert the Great, St. John Mary Vianney, and even Duns Scotus, that they were having very difficult times in college until they turned to the Blessed Mother for learning and wisdom.

Father Hugh Blunt sums up his treatment of this title in this way: "But Jesus has established a university for us in the heart of his Mother. That was his Alma Mater; may it be ours, too."

25

Cause of Our Joy

Hollywood has the uncanny ability, now shared by television, of judging by externals. A case in point is a movie which keeps coming back on late TV. It's entitled *The Bells of St. Mary's* and features Bing Crosby as the irrepressible singing assistant pastor confronted with a convent of nuns. Hollywood sees them as a joyful, mischievous, innocent bunch, rather childish overall.

What they have missed is that Religious tend to be joyful people because of their pursuit of holiness. They are aware of the temptations and hard knocks that life deals out, and they have crosses to carry daily. However, holiness, and the sometimes difficult struggle to attain it, frees the soul from the slavery to sin and give a whole new approach to life. It is a joyful approach.

Now apply this to Mary, and the lesson becomes obvious. She is the cause of our joy not only for the obvious reason that she brought Jesus into the world. There would be no cause for hope or joy without the paschal work of the Holy Redeemer whom she bore.

But Mary is a font of joy because of the work God effected in her soul. Immaculate at her conception, she was bound up in the joy and peace of mind that holiness always brings with it.

The Gospel means "Good News," and Mary is at the heart and soul of the gospel message. An early second-century work, attributed to Barnabas, teaches us: "The Lord has given us three basic doctrines: hope for eternal life, the beginning and end of our faith; justice, the beginning and end of righteousness; and love, which bears cheerful and joyful witness to the works of righteousness."

That Mary understood and radiated this is obvious

from her canticle, the *Magnificat* (Lk 1:46-55). Mary exulted, "My very being proclaims the greatness of the Lord." St. Bernardine of Siena reminds us that Mary is quoted on only seven occasions in the New Testament, and "On all those occasions she spoke very little, except for the one time when the praises of God just poured from her lips. Then she said, 'My soul magnifies the Lord.' But note that here she was speaking to God, not to men."

Mary continues, "My soul finds joy in God my Savior." Benedictine Abbot Columba Marmion writes that "joy is the echo of the God-life in us." The joy that Mary felt was quite literally because of the Christ living in her, both physically and by faith.

Father Kleist translates this verse, "And my spirit leaps for joy in God my Savior." She was ready to leap for joy in the sense of the familiar psalm verse, "Behold, sons are a gift from the Lord; the fruit of the womb is a reward" (Ps 127:3).

Father Kleist translates the next verse as "How graciously he looked upon his lowly maid! Oh, behold, from this hour onward age after age will call me blessed." Mary obviously knows that the source of her joy, and ours, is the gracious work and will of God, a work that will be praised through the centuries.

St. Bede the Venerable remarks, "Truly the Mother of God is blessed that she gave him his flesh, but she is by far the most blessed of all in that her love for him excels for all eternity."

Mary finds joy in the strength of the Almighty who has done these great works in and through her, showing forth not only His mercy but His very holiness. Her joy was nourished through her contact with Christ, as Cardinal Newman says: "She was the witness of his growth, of his joys, of his sorrows, of his prayers; she was blessed with his smile, with the touch of his hand, with the whisper of his affection, with the expression of his thoughts and feelings. . . ."

Again Mary tells us, a cause for joy is the mercy that God shows to the human race. His faithful love extends from age to age to those who fear Him, or as Kleist translates it, "to those who worship him in reverence." The root of the word that is often used in expressions such as "fear of the Lord," can also bear the translation of "in service of the Lord."

True to her Semitic rearing, Mary delights in the paradox that shows the strong and mighty brought low, and the humble and lowly raised up by the power of God. The rich, who are so honored by the world, find that death ends their triumphs, while the humble find life eternal beckoning them.

Finally, Mary rejoices that all the promises made to the Jewish patriarchs, prophets and kings are to be fulfilled in Jesus, her Son. He is the fulfillment of all prophecies, and she has been called to cooperate in God's work.

Yes, her joy had to be full, and devotion to Mary fills us with joy. True devotion to Mary always leads to a better understanding of the role of Jesus Christ, in the reality of the Incarnation of the God-Man.

And even in the sorrows and crosses that are an inevitable part of the human condition, Mary is there as a cause of comfort and perseverance. Her journey along the way of the Cross and her vigilance at the foot of the cross show that her joy was not a shallow, Pollyannaish thing.

It is something like a mother who knows that her child needs a serious operation. The mother feels sympathy for the child, but insists on the operation. The mother sheds tears, but holds the child's hand to give him courage. Then, when the operation is a success, she is properly attentive to all his convalescing needs, but joyful that all is working out well.

So, Christ would have preferred to have passed by Calvary, as He cried out so appealingly in the Garden of Gethsemane, yet, "not my will, but yours be done."

Mary, too, would have just as soon skipped over those episodes. But, "it was necessary for the Christ to suffer death and so enter into his glory." The joy then, was much more triumphant on the first Easter Sunday.

In speaking of the birth of Mary, St. Alphonsus Liguori tells us that "in her nativity, the dawn has appeared. The dawn is the forerunner of the sun, and Mary was the precursor of the Incarnate Word, the Sun of Justice, the Redeemer, who, by his death, delivered us from eternal death.

"With reason the Church sings, 'Your birth, O holy Mother of God, announced joy to the whole world.' And as Mary was the beginning of our joy, so is she also there at its completion, in the work Christ has done."

When commenting on this title, he prays, "O Mother of God, my joy and my hope, you do not deny your favors to anyone, and you obtain whatever you wish from God!"

26

Spiritual Vessel
(Shrine of the Soul)

When the Holy Spirit set St. Paul aside to be the Apostle to the Gentiles, a certain Christian named Ananias was sent to impose hands on him, cure his blindness and baptize him. The Lord himself called Paul "a vessel of election," a chosen instrument (Acts 9:15). In this sense, the three "vessel" invocations indicate that Mary is a very special instrument in the economy of salvation.

First of all, she was the chosen vessel whose womb contained the Lord and brought him into the world. The hymn used in the Common of the Blessed Virgin in *The Liturgy of the Hours* expresses it so beautifully:

> The God whom earth and sea and sky
> Adore and laud and magnify,
> Whose might they own, whose praise they tell,
> In Mary's body deigned to dwell.

> O Mother blest!, the chosen shrine
> Wherein the Architect divine,
> Whose hand contains the earth and sky,
> Vouchsafed in hidden guise to lie:

> Blest in the message Gabriel brought;
> Blest in the work the Spirit wrought;
> Most blest to bring to human birth
> The long desired of all the earth.

> O Lord, the Virgin born, to thee
> Eternal praise and glory be,
> Whom with the Father we adore
> And Holy Spirit for evermore.

All Mariology really boils down to that. When we call Mary "the Mother of God," we have said it all. But like all true lovers, we are never content to look for the least common denominator of our love, but we look for it in all its splendor.

Mary as "Spiritual Vessel" turns our attention to the workings of the Holy Spirit in her soul, and to her special relationship with Him.

With the Old Testament emphasis on the oneness of God, there was no chance for a Trinitarian theology to develop. Yet, when St. Luke records the unique message of the Annunciation — "the Holy Spirit will overshadow you" — Mary accepts this explanation without question.

We have the mystery of the Most Holy Trinity right there, in that passage. God the Father will send God the Holy Spirit to make God the Son incarnate in her womb.

Speak of getting down to the essentials! The Holy Trinity at work in the world, after receiving the consent of the Blessed Virgin Mary!

The equanimity with which Mary receives all this is remarkable, unless there was infused knowledge at that moment. Much more may be implied than the simple recounting of the event.

It is also possible, as St. Alphonsus Liguori teaches, that from the moment of her Immaculate Conception in the womb of Ann, her mother, Mary did have infused knowledge all the time and was aware of the mystery of the Trinity from the very beginning of her existence.

It is also possible that Mary accepted the message in the deepest of faith, and later, as Christ explained this to the Apostles, and after the amazing Pentecost event, she understood it better, or more fully.

Some writers prefer to emphasize the supernatural activity while others try to point out the natural growth in faith and maturity. However, the whole Incarnation event is so completely supernatural that I tend to opt for the more spiritual explanation. Mary was aware of the doctrine of the Holy Trinity more completely than any theologian who attempts to teach about it. When St. Luke narrates the Annunciation story, he is emphasizing her position as the Mother of the Lord.

When he narrates the history of the original Christian Pentecost, he is emphasizing Mary as the Mother of the Church. She is set apart with special dignity in the first Christian community when the Holy Spirit descends for what has so often been called "the birthday of the Church."

St. Gertrude left us a prayer in which she recognizes this relationship between Mary and the Holy Spirit. "O Mother of all blessedness, peerless sanctuary of the Holy Spirit, I praise and greet you through the sweetest Heart of Jesus Christ, the Son of God and your most loving Son; begging you to help us in all our needs and distresses, and at the hour of our death. Amen."

When we speak of Mary as a "spiritual vessel," or sanctuary or temple, we have to remember that her spiritual life was not that of an angel, but of a human being. We get so involved in speaking of her prerogatives and privileges, and we should never tire of doing so, that we forget what a spiritual model she is for all of us.

As Dorothy Day reminds us, Mary's life was taken up with the ordinary duties of a housewife. Hers was the work of cooking and baking and laundry and housecleaning. When our everyday tasks seem insignificant and boring, what a model we have in Mary.

She who talked to angels, perhaps many times in her life, if we can credit many of the spiritual legends, was also responsible for having clean clothes for her two men. She who lived an exalted spiritual life had to plan menus and do the shopping. The private revelations that Mary gave to St. Gertrude and to St. Bridget of Sweden read like chatty, woman-talk conversations.

Mary goes from the most sublime of thoughts to the most common of everyday notions.

She adapts herself to the cultures of the two saints to make her points. She also shows an extraordinary interest in what they have to tell her from their daily lives, both the humble and inspiring.

St. Alphonsus quotes from these two women a great deal in his *Glories of Mary*. He accepted them unquestioningly, although they reflect a culture far different from ours.

The important point, I think, is that Mary does encourage us to bring the homey parts of our prayer life to her. The things that so often distract us in prayer, frequently tell us what is really in our minds and hearts, and therefore what should be the subject of our prayers.

Mary not only bore Christ in her womb. She also bore Him in her heart, that immaculate vessel of immense love. And that Immaculate Heart was not only a spiritual vessel full of love for Jesus, but there is plenty of room in it for all of us.

Baroque Madonna and Child in the Bernini style

27

Vessel of Honor
(Glory of Israel)

When Mary is addressed as the "Vessel of Honor," there can be no doubt that we refer to the honor which God first bestowed on her. In imitating God, we also honor her for a soul so adorned with God's favor that it outshines all the rest of created beauty in excellence.

The new, alternate title, "Glory of Israel," which is simply a new translation of the more ancient title, does shed more light on the honor we should bestow on Mary.

It brings to mind Saul, at whose death David composed a hymn that salutes him as the Glory of Israel. However, King Saul is hardly a good figure of Mary, the Mother of God.

Rather Judith, who saved the Holy City, was saluted by the people as the "Glory of Jerusalem," and in the holy women of the Old Testament, we do have types of Mary.

The Book of Judith, thought by some scholars to be a sort of historical fiction composed to encourage the Jews in their struggles, tells the story of Judith, a youthful widow who lived in the city of Bethulia.

Her city was being besieged by the dreadful and powerful general, Holofernes. Because of the city's strategic importance, the battle for Bethulia is crucial to the war.

The city is on the verge of starvation when Judith, after much prayer, goes into the camp of the enemy and, through an interesting stratagem, manages to be alone with Holofernes and then assassinates him. Leaderless, the enemy falls to the Jews and the invasion is ended.

The priests come from Jerusalem to honor this valiant woman, and they greet her as "the glory of Jerusalem, the surpassing joy of Israel and the splendid boast of the people" (cf. Jdt 15:9).

It is certainly easy for us to apply the moral of this story to Mary. Her faith in God, her complete submission to His will, her bravery, and her cooperation in the work of the redemption of the whole human race make her, indeed, a surpassing joy and a splendid boast. God's grace has completely triumphed in Mary.

She is the glory of Israel, for all that had been promised to patriarchs, kings, priests and prophets has come to fruition through her. Israel, as God's Chosen People, stands as a prophecy of her, for she is the highest fruit of the chosen.

The story of Esther also can be used. The Hebrew maiden Hadassah is chosen to become the Queen of the Persians. She is given the Persian name Esther.

Queen Esther is not particularly attached to being the queen of a pagan nation, and she soon becomes a pawn in a plot between her uncle Mordecai and the king's grand vizier, Haman.

Haman has the king's ear and falsely obtains a decree to exterminate all the Jews. Mordecai reminds Esther that she is included in this decree. After much fasting and prayer, Esther goes to the king and exposes Haman's plot. The Jews are saved from extinction in the kingdom.

Again, the applications to Mary are obvious. Through her prayers and good works, we are saved because she brought Christ the Redeemer into the world. She is a model of prayer and a woman of great faith and charity.

God, as He so frequently does, works His will among mankind by using men, whether they are good or evil. God does not have to resort to miracles, nor does He have to deny free will in guiding events. However, when God uses the Blessed Mother, He uses the fairest flower of our race. It is no wonder that her intercession is so powerful.

Mary lived in a society which accorded women few rights. Yet, she came at the end of a long line of holy and valiant women who left their marks on the Old Testament world.

She may also have been the model that Our Lord used in the many parables involving women. How often He must have watched His Mother when she made bread and used leaven. Did she sweep the house, looking for a lost coin that would have been so precious to a poor family? And the story of the wise and foolish virgins, did that stem from her?

The jugs of water, those common water vessels used at Cana of Galilee, must have been familiar to Jesus. Probably He had brought water to their little home many times. Common as they were, He made them famous through His first public miracle.

The idea of a vessel, then, would naturally fit into our thinking about Mary. That she would be honorable is a most natural conclusion. In fact, the holier a person is, the more pleasing he or she is to God. Since Mary rightly has the title of holiest among all of mankind, what is more logical than to salute Mary as the most honorable vessel.

The great artists of the past were attracted to her sanctity, and some of the greatest masterpieces are their attempt to honor her with their best work. Without exhausting the subject at all, St. Paul Editions published a large art book titled *The Life of the Madonna in Art*.

In almost 200 pages of pictures and text, with the reproductions mostly in vivid color, some of the works of the greatest painters are displayed. They include Fra Angelico, Bellini, Botticelli, Caravaggio, Donatello, Giotto, Da Vinci, Michelangelo, Raphael, Titian and many others. They are united in trying to give glory to God by honoring this special vessel of election, Mary.

The story is told, and I cannot prove it, about the "secret" Christians of Japan who treasured their faith for almost three centuries while priests were not allowed into the country. Just before World War I, missionaries were again allowed into that nation.

These secret believers watched patiently as the priests learned the language and went about their activities. They were convinced that the missionaries were preaching the Christ that had been handed down to them, but, did they belong to the True Church, the Church Christ had founded? Finally, they approached the priests with three questions.

Are you obedient to the Holy Father in Rome? Are your priests unmarried? Do you honor the Mother of God? The affirmative answer showed that these were, indeed, Catholic missionaries.

It doesn't surprise us at all that honoring Mary should be one of the practical marks of the Church. We cannot repeat it often enough — God first honored her with the fullness of grace.

28

Singular Vessel of Devotion (Vessel of Selfless Devotion)

St. Bede the Venerable wrote a particularly beautiful homily on the eleventh chapter of St. Luke's Gospel. He describes the impression that Christ's teachings were having on the common people, as opposed to the pride of the Scribes and Pharisees.

One listener, a woman, cries out, "Blessed is the womb that bore you and the breasts that nursed you!" St. Bede says, "He was actually formed in and from the woman's virginal womb. His flesh was not created out of nothing, nor made from some foreign material. He is the flesh and blood of his Mother.

"Otherwise, he would not be the Son of Man because he would have had no origin from man. Let us indeed join the woman of this Gospel passage in her praise. Let us reflect the voice of the Catholic Church when it condemned the heretics and let us sing out above the crowd, 'Blessed is the womb that bore you and the breasts that nursed you!'

"Blessed indeed is the Mother of whom it has been said, 'She has given birth to the king who rules Heaven and earth forever.'

" 'But even more blessed,' responds the Savior, 'are those who hear the word of God and act upon it.' He graciously acknowledges her praise. He points out that not only is Mary blessed because she gave him birth according to the flesh, but that she and all others are blessed who bring him forth by good works and nourish him by their own lives and by sharing their faith with others.

"Truly the Mother is blessed that she gave him his flesh, but she is by far the most blessed of all in that her love for him excels for all eternity." That expresses so beautifully what this title of the Litany means. Mary is unique in that her own devotion to God is so complete, so thorough and so entirely selfless.

She is the Model of Devotion for all mankind. Her faith, hope and charity are all that God could ask of her, and they fulfill the high destiny and the fullness of grace bestowed on her by God. Mother of God!

"Devotion," as St. Thomas Aquinas teaches, "consists in the readiness with which our will conforms itself to the will of God." That was the principle which made Mary so dear to God.

That was how Our Lord meant His reply to the woman in the gospel passage to be understood. Mary was more blessed by the union of her will with that of God than by being His Mother.

As the sunflower, we are told, always points its blossom toward the sun, so, says St. Alphonsus Liguori, "the divine will was alone the aim and satisfaction of the heart of Mary, as she herself proclaimed, 'My spirit rejoices in God my Savior!' "

Devotion is a spontaneous response, and as such it plays upon the emotions. Real devotion must be nourished by a firm grasp of the truths of our faith so that it is not merely emotional or hysterical.

St. Ignatius Loyola grasped this in the *Spiritual Exercises*. The soul must confront the ultimate reasons for existence and face them fearlessly. One has to grasp how powerless and inane is man without God, yet with God, all things are possible.

The immense theological facts of the Incarnation and the Redemption must be understood as much as possible, and they they must be found attractive and applicable. Then, and only then, can devotion be spurred on. It has a rock-solid base to start from.

Notice that St. Ignatius puts great emphasis on the Passion and death of Christ. The Crucifixion was the way that He *had to use* to enter into His glory. This is what Our Lord told those two special disciples on the Road to Emmaus: "Oh how foolish you are. How slow of heart to believe all that the prophets spoke. Was it not necessary that the Messiah should suffer these things and enter into his glory?" (Lk 24:25-26).

Mary did not even hesitate when she followed her Son on what the *Imitation of Christ* calls "the royal road of the Cross"! Her devotion was firmly grounded on the truths that underlay our economy of salvation. Indeed, she was a part of them, at the very start of them in human history and, we may add, at the heart of them.

And her Immaculate Heart was purified during those terrible, awe-ful hours of the first Good Friday.

St. Bernardine of Siena reminds us of these facts: "With what words shall I, a mere man, express the tremendous love of that virginal heart, when even the tongues of all the angels would not suffice. The Lord has said that the good man brings forth good things from the treasure of the heart, and this saying can also be a treasure.

"Among all the human race, who can even be thought of as purer than she who merited to become the Mother of God, who for nine months had God as her Guest in her heart and in her womb? What greater treasure is there than divine Love Himself, burning in the Heart of this Virgin as in a furnace?

"From her heart as from a furnace of Divine Love, the Blessed Virgin spoke the words of the most ardent love. Since from a vessel of good rich wine only good wine can be poured, and from a burning furnace only great heat can come, so from Mary Christ can receive only the words of ardent love."

Allusion to the Immaculate Heart of Mary is mentioned from time to time by the Fathers and Doctors of the Church, and Mary's heart is mentioned twice in the Gospels. However, the honor of really giving impetus to this devotion must go to St. John Eudes in the seventeenth century. From that time on, and usually in conjunction with devotion to the Sacred Heart of Jesus, the Catholic imagination turned to the Immaculate Heart of Mary with great fervor.

Then the apparitions at Fatima during World War I and finally the consecration of Russia and the world to the Immaculate Heart of Mary by Pope Pius XII in World War II bought it to its present prominence.

In need, a child turns to its mother. And that Mother, a model of selfless devotion herself, teaches us how to be better and more mature Christians. In the words of St. Alphonsus: "You are blessed, my Lady, who always and in all ways were united to the divine will. Obtain for me the grace to spend the rest of my life in constant conformity to the will of God."

29

Mystical Rose

The theology of St. Augustine was so thoroughly God-directed that he frequently leaves the impression of emphasizing the spiritual to the exclusion of the human. Like St. John the Evangelist, his love of Christ was so overpowering that he seemed to view everything else as of little or no importance.

Modern Western civilization has become so humanistic that it denies the power and richness of the spiritual in the glorification of Man. With that reversal of priorities, there have come more destructive wars than mankind has ever known and a cheapening of human values to the point that abortion and euthanasia are very tenable positions. Economic power has been vested in the few and the masses suffer more than ever before. The Holocaust by the Nazis and the Atomic Bomb have put permanent scars on this century.

Dante, whom some have called the "first modern man," seemed to find the partnership between the spiritual and the temporal that gives each the importance that is its due. The city of God and the city of man deal with the same citizens and each has a proper role, supportive of the other, for the common good and the promotion of the individual's rights.

Dante's views, as expressed in the *Divine Comedy*, show the role of reason, personified in the poet Virgil, and the role of charity, personified in Beatrice. Unaided reason can take us just so far, then Christian charity directs us to Paradise.

At the height of Paradise, around the throne of the Deity, are the angels and the souls of the saints, arrayed as the petals of a mystical rose that gives glory to God. And as Dante concludes his poetic vision, so firmly grounded in the theology of St. Thomas Aquinas, St. Bernard comes to tell Dante how important Mary is as the Mother of God.

Speaking of Mary, Dante says, "Here is the Rose wherein the Word Divine was made Incarnate," and he has St. Bernard explain, "The saints are, in graduation, throned on the rose, when at the name of that fair flower, whom daily I invoke both morn and eve, my soul with all her might collected, on the goodliest arbor fixed."

That Mary herself would be designated as the Mystical Rose, whose beauty leads us to God, whose fragrance attracts our souls to Christ as bees are attracted to rose blossoms, would fit right in to Dante's views of Mary's commanding role in the economy of salvation.

Msgr. John Portman, a priest friend of mine, once referred to a rose in a homily as "the most beautiful flower God has ever created." To this, we must add the title of Jesuit Father John M. Scott's book, that *Without Thorns, It's Not a Rose* (Our Sunday Visitor Books).

For Mary, the mystical rose, the most beautiful human being God has ever created, knew also the thorns of sorrow. Hers is not an ethereal beauty set apart from reality. No one shared in the sufferings of Christ to the degree that Mary did and she offered these along with Him with a full and generous heart.

In the Wisdom literature of the Old Testament, the Church, especially through the Liturgy, delights in attributing so many of the references to Our Lady. Certainly all the verses praising or using flowers for symbols are applied to Mary.

In the Canticle of Canticles we read "My sister, my spouse, is a garden enclosed" (Sg 4:12), "As the lily among thorns, so is my love among the daughters" (Sg 2:2), and "I to my beloved and my beloved to me who feeds among the lilies" (Sg 6:3).

In the Book of Sirach we find, "As the vine I have

brought forth a pleasant odor; and my flowers are the first of honor and riches" (24:23), "In me is all grace of the way and of the truth; in me is all hope of life and of virtue" (24:25), and "As a rose planted by the waters have I budded forth. . . Send forth flowers, as the lily, and yield a smell, and bring forth leaves in grace and praise with songs and bless the Lord in his work" (39:17,19). This same book also contains, "I was exalted like a palm tree in Cades and as a rose plant in Jericho" (24:18).

As St. Bernard exclaims, "Christ who willed to be conceived and reared in Nazareth finds his delight in flowers!" He adds that "Our Lord planted all the flowers which adorn the Church in this garden (the soul of Mary); and amongst others, the violet of humility, the lily of purity and the rose of charity."

St. Alphonsus Liguori offers this opinion. A rose is red and of a fiery color which denotes love of God and of our neighbor, therefore, on account of the ardent love with which the heart of Mary was always inflamed toward God and us, she is rightly called "a rose."

While our devotion allows us to use the symbol of the modern rose as a sign of Mary, many of these biblical flowers were a far cry from today's award-winners. Some of them were wild flowers, or narcissus, or flax or even the scarlet anemone. Devotion does not stumble over this bit of information.

Thus, the ancient Irish author Sedulius could expound, "And as the rose all soft and beautiful comes forth from the thorny stem, without offense to the parent stock its lovely blossom shades, so from the race of sinful Eve, Mary, a sacred Virgin, comes forth, glowing with sacred light, wiping out the fault of the first virgin."

It is safe to say that Our Lady must have loved flowers, since she loved all of God's creation. In many of her private revelations to mankind, she has appeared with, or used flowers.

The devotion to Our Lady of the Snows commemorates roses found in the middle of snow on a hilltop in Rome in the month of August, to designate where the first Marian church was to be built in that city. At Lourdes, she wore a golden rose on each foot.

Roses figure prominently in the story of Guadalupe. On Saturday, December 9, 1531, while Juan Diego was hurrying to Mass in Mexico City, Our Lady appeared to him and told him to ask the bishop to build her a shrine on that spot. Naturally, the bishop demanded a sign.

Our Lady appeared again and directed Juan Diego to a rocky spot where she told him to gather roses. It was a most unlikely spot, but he went, and sure enough there were roses there. Our Lady arranged them in the Indian's cloak and told him to take them, undisturbed, to the bishop. When Juan opened his cloak in the presence of the bishop and his people, the shower of roses fell out and there, on the cloak was the glorious picture of the Mother of God. It is still venerated at her shrine in Mexico City.

The word "mystical" here means secret or hidden. Thus, the Christian Sacraments are called "mysteries," because they have a powerful, spiritual force far beyond the sign that appears to the senses. So, the beauty of Mary's soul and the power of her intercession, symbolized by the rose, go far beyond the appearances.

And so we sang, in our youth, in a hymn which is still heard at May crownings:

Bring flowers of the fairest
Bring flowers of the rarest
From hillside and valley
And mountain and dale. . . .
O Mary we crown you with blossoms today,
Queen of the Angels, Queen of the May. . . .

30

Tower of David

This prophetic title takes its origin from the Song of Songs, "Your neck is like David's tower, girt with battlements; A thousand bucklers hang upon it, all the shields of valiant men" (Sg 4:4).

Until the use of dynamite became a part of warfare, the tower of a city was its main defense and a place where watchmen could warn of impending dangers. A city or a town with a strong wall, heavy gates, towers, steady water supply, and food stocks could withstand a siege and sorty out at will.

Even before that, as we read in Scripture and know from archeology, towers were used to protect oases with their invaluable and precious water, flocks, and crops.

That Mary should be symbolized as a tower can come as no surprise. We saw that the Church, in defining her divine maternity at the Council of Ephesus, was actually guaranteeing the doctrine of the Incarnation. Jesus Christ, the Second Person of the Blessed Trinity, is both true God and true man. He has both natures, the one from His Father, the other from His mother, Mary.

Where true devotion to Mary languishes, understanding of the Son soon withers. It lacks all the fullness of the rich, Catholic Tradition and custom. Like the Magi, we will find the Child with His mother.

The Protestant reformers were right in rejecting some of the excessive devotions of their day, but they erred egregiously in denying almost all devotion to Mary. They were soon racked from within by an almost infinite variety of Christological and ecclesiastical errors and divided up into countless sects.

Mary is correctly called a tower for the defense of the Faith. She continues to protect her Son as she did throughout all the days of Bethlehem, Egypt, and Nazareth. Now her sons and daughters are spread throughout the world, and she continues to be a tower of strength for us.

Naming her the Tower of David is most apt. She was told by the archangel St. Gabriel, "Behold, you will conceive in your womb and bear a son, and you shall name him Jesus. He will be great and will be called Son of the Most High, and the Lord God will give him the throne of David his father, and he will rule over the house of Jacob forever, and of his kingdom there will be no end" (Lk 1:31-33).

Where was the throne of David? Where, indeed, was the House of David? Rome ruled this poverty-stricken province almost with contempt, and certainly with tyranny and taxation. They changed the nominal rulers, kinglets and princes, at will. The high priesthood was being traded around, year by year.

Almost against hope, and in the face of historical impossibilities, people like St. Joseph and Mary believed that God would be true to His promises. In fact, in her *Magnificat* (Lk 1:46-55) Mary exults in the fact that God was now fulfilling His promises and prophecies.

She proved herself a knowledgeable and loyal Jewess, looking back at the covenants made with Abraham, Isaac, and Jacob, "according to his promise to our fathers."

That her Son would inherit the throne of David was a certainty for her. That it would be the spiritual power and be truly everlasting was all a bonus for the whole human race.

The saints loved to salute Mary, the Mother of the Lord, as a true Jewess, the Daughter of Zion, the descendant of the Patriarchs, starting with Abraham. God's promise of an everlasting king of the line of David depended for its fulfillment on Mary's lineage, literally, and Joseph's descent legally.

In David's time, the King united church and state in his own person. As Christ pointed out, His Kingdom was not of this world, so He was establishing the spiritual kingdom, forever.

One of the very first post-Apostolic writers was St. Ignatius of Antioch. In his letter to the Ephesians he declares, "Come together in common, one and all without exception, in charity, in one faith, and in one Jesus Christ, who is of the race of David according to the flesh, the son of man and the Son of God, so that with undivided mind you may obey the bishop and the priests, and break one Bread which is the medicine of immortality, and the audience against death, enabling us to live forever in Jesus Christ."

Another second-century document, a letter attributed to a certain Barnabas, also alludes to the fulfillment of this prophecy: "See again Jesus, not as son of man, but as Son of God, manifested by a type in the flesh. So, since they will say that Christ is David's son, David himself prophesies, fearing and realizing the error of sinners, 'The Lord said to my Lord, "Sit at my right hand until I make your enemies your footstool" (Ps 110:1). . . . See how David calls him Lord and does not say Son.'"

St. Bernard contributes, "Truth has finally returned to the earth, not through angelic creatures but through this daughter of Abraham. Great as the angels are who minister to God, Mary far surpasses them, for she has been chosen not as servant, but as Mother."

Novatian, writing on the Trinity, says, "Therefore, let those who read in the Scripture that the man Christ Jesus is the Son of God, also read there that this same Jesus is called both God and Son of God.

"In the same manner that he, as man, is of Abraham, even so as God, is he also before Abraham himself.

"In the same manner that he, as man, is the Son of David, so he is also, as God, called the Lord of David."

St. Bernardine of Siena points out that the tower that David built on Mount Zion to protect Jerusalem stood on a very high peak. Mary is called the Tower of David to signify the height of perfection of this great creature. "As Zion was a very elevated spot, so was the Blessed Virgin most exalted."

Just as from a tower, the watchman can keep one eye on all the actions around a city, so Mary, as the Tower of David, can sum up all the prophetic longings of the Old Testament in her soul, and look forward into the New Testament to see her Son begin His reign.

In her life and love, the Old and the New are bridged.

31
Tower of Ivory

"Your neck is like a tower of ivory.
Your eyes are like the pools in Heshbon
by the gate of Bath-rabbim.
Your nose is like the tower on Lebanon
that looks towards Damascus" (Sg 7:5).

The Groom describes his Beloved in the Song of
Songs in a manner that is natural to lovers of every
time and place. She has all the attributes of beauty,
and everything beautiful reminds him of her.

It is no wonder, then, that the Church applies these
verses to the Blessed Mother. God has created nothing
more beautiful. Her soul is the most perfect dwelling
place of the Holy Trinity that can be found among creatures.

Ivory, today, is something precious and we remark
at the beautiful things that can be carved from it. It
had a special fascination for the ancients, and the Jews
were no exception. It is mentioned a dozen times in the
Old Testament, and once in the New Testament.

Solomon, with all his wisdom and splendor, was
also a shrewd businessman and a consummate
politician. He sent ships all over the Near East and
traded in gold, silver, ivory, and art objects (1 Kgs
10:22). He made Jerusalem the trade crossroads of his
time, and he prospered accordingly.

As a politician, he knew how important it was that
he give the right impression. Today we'd call it PR
(public relations) savvy. The temple he built was one of
the wonders of the ancient world, and his palace and
possessions made the Queen of Sheba gasp in wonder.

He had a precious throne made, carved of ivory and
inlaid with gold. So much ivory was used in his palace

that it was actually called a palace of ivory. Naturally, the wealthy men of the land followed suit and used ivory extensively.

When the Psalmist wanted to indicate the luxury of the period, he sang "from ivory palaces string music brings you joy" (Ps 45:9).

When the luxury turned to decadence and a falling away from God, the prophets denounced those living in the ivory palaces and foretold their utter destruction.

The Book of Revelation describes some of the furnishing of the new Babylon (Imperial Rome) that would be destroyed by God's wrath for their persecution of the People of God (Rv 18:12).

In Mary Immaculate, there is no fading or spoiling possible in the beauty in her soul. Cardinal Newman tells us that "she is called the Tower of Ivory to suggest to us, by the brightness, purity and exquisiteness of that material, how transcendent is the loveliness and the gentleness of the Mother of God."

In nature, beauty is everywhere if we have the insight to recognize it. Artists so often look at the most ordinary sights and find a beauty to paint that goes beyond us ordinary mortals. And then, when they have finished a particularly beautiful work, they feel that it is inadequate. It doesn't begin to express all they see in it.

In his book *The Thirteenth: the Greatest of Centuries*, James J. Walsh devotes a whole chapter to the origin of the great European art and artists, starting with Cimabue. The Madonnas of that period are smiling, human, and natural. They express the love of God and neighbor in their faces.

Cimabue's most famous Madonna, still on view in Florence, was the object of a special visit by King Charles of Anjou, and it was borne in a triumphant procession from the artist's studio to the Church of Santa Maria Novella.

Giotto, the greatest artist of the thirteenth century

according to Walsh, produced a life of Christ for Padua through the fourteen episodes in the life of His Mother. He sought to express spiritual beauty through true natural beauty.

Since there is true beauty in physical nature, it is even more true in human nature, because we were created in the image and likeness of God. When God created Eve, she was a perfect expression of God's idea of feminine beauty, especially with the pristine grace in her soul.

All that Eve could have been, is found in its fullness in Mary. That was promulgated to the whole world by the glorious "Ave!" of Gabriel, and sealed by the whole-hearted *fiat* of Mary. And the Church responds, "Who is she that approaches as a brilliant dawn, fair as the moon, bright as the sun, terrible as an army drawn up for battle!"

St. Bernard remarks, "Know, O man, the plan of God. Recognize the plan of his wisdom, the counsel of his love. The price of universal salvation has been given us through Mary, that she might retrieve the reputation of our first mother, Eve."

And St. Augustine contributes, in his tribute to the feast of the nativity of Mary, "The miraculous new birth has conquered the cause of grief. Mary's song of praise quiets the mourning of Eve."

Mary, the New Eve, Immaculate from the first instant of her conception, was definitely the height of God's creation. Christian artists of every century and school have tried to portray their ideas of Mary, and they always include their finest ideals of beauty.

Sculptors have done their best to praise Mary's beauty, as have architects who have placed their shrines, churches, cathedrals, and basilicas in the forefront of devotion to Mary.

Most beautiful of all, of course, was the triumph of grace in Mary's soul. "All during her life" writes Jesuit Father Albert Power, "God was perfecting her soul by the activity of His grace, building up the incomparable Tower of Ivory that was to be pre-eminently the palace of His residence forever."

Because of the beauty of her soul, the Church applies the words of Psalm 87:3 to her: "Glorious things are said of you, O city of God," and also the words from Revelation 21:2: "I saw the Holy City, the New Jerusalem, coming down out of heaven from God, prepared as a bride adorned to meet her husband."

We most resemble Mary if we allow the Holy Spirit to carry out the works of grace in our souls, so that we, too, adorned and prepared to meet the Bridegroom when the time comes for us to die, are made ready for eternal life and love.

St. Alphonsus comments on the whole phrase from the Canticle which gives rise to this title: "Thus is Mary called 'Thy neck is a tower of ivory.' Mary is called a neck; for she is the mystic neck through which the vital spirits, that is, the divine help which preserves in us the life of grace, are transmitted from Jesus Christ, the head to us the faithful, who are members of the mystic Body of Christ."

St. Bernardine of Siena says that "the life-giving graces flow from Christ the Head, through the Blessed Virgin, into his mystical Body." And he adds that "from the time when Mary conceived the Incarnate Word, she received great honor from God, that no one should receive any grace otherwise than through her hands (from Jesus)."

The bosom of Mary has been called "an ivory tower of unspeakable delights." What an inspiration it is for us to know that one day we shall find our safety and peace through that fortress of the Tower of Ivory!

32

House of Gold

How appropriate this beautiful title is to the Mother of God. It is a scriptural reference to the Temple of Solomon, and rightly applied to her who was Christ's first human temple.

Gold has always had a fascination for humans, and from ancient to contemporary times, gold is the ultimate basis of exchange. How many people follow the price of gold today in the money markets of the world.

How many people rushed to California in the 1850s to make their fortune in gold. The story of The Lost Dutchman, that legendary gold strike whose location was hidden so carefully that men still dream of finding it, motivates prospectors even now.

The lust for gold and silver drove the Spanish *Conquistadores* to conquer almost two whole continents and many other lands. Pharaohs of Egypt and emperors of Rome surrounded themselves with it, and the story of King Croesus is itself a legend.

So it is right and fitting that the Temple that Solomon built to the glory of Yahweh was so filled with and covered with the precious metal that it was called the House of Gold. We are told that when foreign visitors came to Jerusalem, they were lost in awe at its magnificence.

The sixth chapter of the First Book of Kings (formerly Kgs III) details some of that splendor. The inner sanctuary, the Holy of Holies, was completely overlaid with gold. Even nails of gold were used to fasten the gold plates to the walls.

Nothing was too good for the service of their God.

The statues of the two winged Cherubim in the inner Temple, where much of the daily worship occurred, were overlaid with gold and so was the floor.

There was a golden altar, and all the instruments of worship were of gold. (It is interesting to note that the same book in the Old Testament that forbade "graven images," commanded that the two statues of the Cherubim be placed in the Holy of Holies.)

As one entered the more public places in the Temple, gold was in evidence, as well as other precious metals, in great abundance. Shields of gold decorated the walls and the front entrance. The value in today's market is just unimaginable.

And the parallel between the splendor of God's Temple and Mary as the Temple of God is delightfully easy to draw. Nothing is too good for the service of God, so the love and beauty of Mary's soul are simply indescribably beautiful.

The poet, Father John W. Lynch tries to tell us about it in his epic poem, *A Woman Wrapped in Silence*. He pictures the Holy Family at Bethlehem just after the birth of the Child:

"And then,
She knelt and held Him close against her heart,
And in the midnight, adoration fused
With human love, and was not separate.
And very near, the man named Joseph came.
He was not tired now, nor worn, nor sad.
His step was gentle, and a lightness soared
Within him till the memory of
Angel voices heard in dreams was now a less
Remembrance for him than the sight of hands
That held a sleeping child.
He was the first
to find her thus, the first of all the world. . . ."

"Adoration fused with human love. . . ." Who but a poet could put the two together so significantly. The love in Mary's soul was more precious than all the precious metals in the man-built temple. This was a

Temple, a House of Gold, not built by man, but formed by the power of the Holy Spirit in her who was "full of grace."

The Christian heart can continue this parallel, since the Temple in Jerusalem, rebuilt by Herod in Christ's lifetime, has great significance in Christ's life.

Father John L. McKenzie in the *Dictionary of the Bible* gives his usual brilliant but brief look at this. The Gospels show us that Jesus was often in the Temple, and from the age of twelve He took part in the public worship.

The loss of the Child Jesus on that occasion was one of the great Sorrows of Mary, even as finding Him after three days became one of the Joyful Mysteries of the Rosary. What close neighbors bitter sorrow and open joy can be!

Even before that, at the Presentation of the Child Jesus in the Temple, we have that combination of joy and sorrow (Lk 2:22-38). The Holy Family came in humbly, joyfully, to offer the sacrifice of the poor. They would have been indistinguishable from the many other families there that day to perform this joyful duty, so full of promise, so rich in prophesy fulfilled.

But Simeon would make his own prophecy, of the sword of sorrow that would pierce Mary's heart. Our Lady told St. Bridget of Sweden that that prophecy was with her vividly for the rest of her life, until Calvary.

During His Public Life, Jesus often taught in the Temple and, He called it His Father's House, the house of God and a house of prayer. The episode of the cleansing of the Temple from the money-changers is recounted in all four Gospels.

He used the Temple as a symbol of His own body: "Destroy this Temple and in three days I will restore it" (Jn 2:14-17). This has further implications for us since the Church was soon to be identified with the Body of Christ, He being the Head, we the members.

Since Mary was never far from Him during His

public ministry, it is safe to assume that she, too, was familiar with the Temple precincts, insofar as they were open to women. She knew His love for this visible symbol of the covenant between His Father and His people, Israel.

Mary understood the reality behind the symbolism. She knew that, through the Incarnation, all this was passing over to a higher form of worship. She who could well sing with the Psalmist, "The law of your mouth is to me more precious than thousands of gold and silver pieces" (Ps 119:72), was herself a more precious Temple and a more sacred and loving dwelling-place of her Son, the Temple's Lord.

St. Albert the Great calls her a "golden Temple of charity," and his disciple, St. Thomas Aquinas adds, "as all in the Temple was covered with gold, so was everything in the beautiful soul of Mary filled with sanctity."

Mary our Mother, saluted in song as "our life, our sweetness and our hope," has all the treasury of God at her disposal. We are the children of the Queen, the brothers and sisters of her only Son, Jesus Christ. Surely she will never see our souls in want, nor be indifferent to our temporal needs. She longs to share her richness with us.

Mary is the House of Gold which Eternal Wisdom, that is the Divine Word, chose for His dwelling on earth, as it is said, "Wisdom has built herself a house" (Prv 9:1).

And, marvelous to relate, we are invited to dwell with her in her House of Gold!

33

Ark of the Covenant

One of the most majestic titles given to the Blessed Mother is this one, "Ark of the Covenant," — one that is so rich in imagery and wonder.

The actual Ark of the Covenant, from biblical history, was the oblong box or chest in which were placed the Ten Commandments, as recorded by Moses after he had dashed the original two stones against the ground upon finding Aaron's golden calf being worshiped.

It was constructed of acacia wood, or setim, a wood so hard as to be almost indestructible. It was covered with gold, inside and out.

According to many sources, the Ark also contained a pot of manna and the rod of Aaron that had been used miraculously in Egypt and during the Exodus.

The Ark was carried along the journey to the Holy Land to show that Yahweh was the Leader of the people. It was carried into battle to invoke His powerful intercession, and it was later enshrined in the Holy of Holies of the Temple of Solomon, to symbolize the presence of God in the Temple.

In the Holy of Holies, it was surmounted by a gold ledge, called the Mercy Seat or the Propitiatory. Overshadowing all this were the statues of the two golden cherubim. From this Mercy Seat God would dispense mercy and knowledge to the people through the priests.

The Ark was lost to history at the time of the destruction of the Temple by Nebuchadnezzar in 586 B.C. Whether it was destroyed, or taken captive, or hidden by the priests, is disputed by the experts.

In the earliest Christian Fathers, the Ark became a symbol of Christ Himself. Both St. Thomas Aquinas and St. Bonaventure in the Middle Ages still used that terminology, especially seeing the manna contained in

Ark as a symbol of Jesus Christ in the Eucharist.

However, many of the titles from Old Testament symbols, while directed to Christ primarily, were frequently applied to Mary as well. The Marian symbolism of this title almost speaks for itself, and in our times this is an almost exclusive Marian title in Christian usage.

The incorruptible wood is a ready-made figure of Mary Immaculate, totally preserved from the corruption of sin from the instant of her conception in her mother's womb.

The gold that covered the Ark inside and out were a symbol of the tremendous graces and overflowing charity in Mary's soul, which was truly a House of Gold, so precious in the sight of God.

Over the top of the Ark was the Propitiatory, or Mercy Seat. The virtue of mercy has been especially connected with devotion to Mary for many, many centuries. St. Alphonsus composed the first part of his *Glories of Mary* as a very lengthy commentary on the prayer *Hail Holy Queen, Mother of Mercy*. According to him, Mary is that Mercy Seat, through whose hands God dispenses His mercy to us.

Surrounding the Ark were the gold statues of the two cherubim, those great angelic spirits who might well remind us of St. Michael and St. Gabriel, being of service to the Queen of Angels.

Father Hugh Blunt adds, "The Ark was the Shrine for the Tables of the Lord; Mary was the Shrine for the Giver of the Law." It was the repository for the rod of Aaron which had blossomed; Mary was the fair lily of Israel. It was the tabernacle for the jar of Manna that had fallen from heaven; Mary was the tabernacle for *Emmanuel*, God with us, the God of the Eucharist.

When Moses first placed the Ark in his tent, God filled it with His glory and covered it with a cloud. Similar powerful experiences occurred when the Ark was brought into Jerusalem, and when it was finally enshrined in the permanent Temple built by Solomon.

At the Annunciation, when the Word became flesh in Mary's womb, the Incarnation occurred when Mary was overshadowed with the power of the Holy Spirit.

The Ark was the visible pledge that God would be with His people to guide them and to give them victory over their enemies. Mary is God's special pledge to us that by her intercession we can triumph over the enemies of sin and faithlessness.

An ancient Latin hymn puts these words on our lips: "O Mother, you are blessed by the gift of the Ark to whose womb was enclosed the heavenly Creator who holds the universe in the hollow of his hand."

Hesychius, a fifth-century Palestinian monk who made notable contributions to Mariology, such as his insistence on her remaining virgin, even *in partu*, in actual childbirth, calls her the "Ark of the Word Incarnate."

He adds, "The Ark of your sanctification is surely the Virgin *Theotokos*. If you, Lord, are the pearl then she must be the Ark." And further, "The truly royal Ark, the most precious Ark, was the ever-Virgin *Theotokos*; the Ark which received the treasure of all sanctification...."

The notion of Mary as the true Ark of the New Testament grew steadily with many references to it, including ones by St. Albert the Great, St. Anthony of Padua and St. Lawrence of Brindisi. It culminated in the use by Pope Pius XII in the Apostolic Constitution *Munificentissimus Deus*:

"... Some of the Fathers have employed the words of the Psalmist: 'Arise, O Lord, and go into your resting place, you and the Ark of your might' (Ps 132:8) and have looked upon the Ark of the Covenant, built of incorruptible wood and placed in the Lord's temple, as a type of the most pure body of the Virgin Mary, preserved and exempted from all corruption of the tomb and raised up to such glory in heaven."

St. Alphonsus Liguori adds another dimension to the title, perhaps forcing a little too much into it, but certainly adding an interesting second dimension. He refers this also to Noah's Ark.

Mary is an Ark more spacious than Noah's, since in Noah's Ark only two animals of every kind are saved, but under Mary's mantle all, both the just and repentant sinners, find place.

St. Gertrude was granted a private revelation in which she saw a multitude of wild beasts take refuge under Mary's mantle. She did not drive them away, but by her gentleness she won them over. The animals that entered Noah's Ark remained animals; repentant sinners who are received by Mary are brought to true repentance and returned to God.

With reverence and love, then, let us approach Mary, the true Ark of the Covenant, the Ark of the testimony of God's presence with us, the pledge to us of God's help. With this Ark leading us, we will never be defeated.

34

Gate of Heaven

For the most part, in our times, gates are pretty ornamental things that give entrance to fences around gardens and homes. However, in security conscious areas, they can be formidable obstructions with gatekeepers to determine who will pass through.

This is one of its most popular uses in the Scriptures. The gate itself frequently symbolizes the whole structure being protected. The Israelites, for instance, are promised that they will be strong enough to "take possession of the gates of their enemies" (Gn 22:17).

When a place is singularly well-protected, it is described in terms such as "fortified with high walls and gates and bars" (Dt 3:5). A well-protected place would be a "walled city with gates barred with bronze" (1 Kgs 4:13).

The principle gates of a city would usually open into a market and meeting place, and it was here the elders gathered to discuss weighty matters and render decisions. There was more consensual democracy than is usually presumed.

The same was true of the royal gates of palaces, where there was room for military display, gatherings to hear pronouncements, and a place for suppliants to gather. Gates play an important part of the main story in the book of Esther and Judith.

Our Lord uses this symbolism often. He warns His followers that the gate to damnation is wide and the road attractive, while narrow is the gate that leads to life eternal (Mt 7:13-14).

The poignant story of Dives and Lazarus revolves around the beggar who sat at the gate. The only son of the widow of Naim, whom Christ restored to life, was a drama that took place at the city gate (Lk 7:11ff).

And what would the story of the Good Shepherd be without the setting of a devoted shepherd who knows his sheep, lets them out the gates of the sheepfold, and guards them with his life, or goes off into the wild seeking the errant.

In Matthew 16:18, when St. Peter is declared the human vicar of Christ, that Church, founded by Christ on the rock of Peter is to triumph over the gates of hell.

These are some of the ideas gathered into the beautiful Marian title Gate of Heaven. She is that powerful intercessor who comes to the defense of her beleaguered clients, beset by spiritual and temporal enemies. St. Alphonsus Liguori reminds us that so powerful are her prayers that God refuses her nothing that she asks.

The widow at Naim did not ask Christ for a miracle. He gave it unasked. So those who are devout clients of Mary do not even have to ask. Mary as Mother knows what we need better than we do ourselves.

Poor human nature stands like a beggar at the gates of Heaven, and our very poverty cries out to Jesus and Mary for help in our needs. Like Lazarus, the Christian in death wants to be received into Heaven amidst the joy of those who love and serve the great Christ the King and His Blessed Mother.

We have seen that Mary as *Theotokos*, Mother of God and Mother of the Church, is the strong protectress against all heresies. All of them wither before her, since as Mother of God she embodies the truth of the Incarnation.

The one biblical prophecy, however, from which this title is probably taken directly comes from the 28th chapter of the Book of Genesis and the story of Jacob (Israel).

In a dream Jacob saw the angels of God on a ladder which reached to Heaven, ascending and descending. The Lord promised him that in his seed all the nations of the earth should be blessed. When Jacob awoke, he said, "How terrible is this place! This is no other than the House of God and Gate of Heaven." He named the site Bethel, "the House of God," and it became the place of the first public worship in the Holy Land.

Through Mary, Christ descended to the earth. She became the "Ladder of Heaven," as the old Irish phrase has it, and for us, the gateway into heaven's treasuries.

If the twenty gates of the city of Jerusalem speak of all these symbolic ideas, the gates of the Temple built by Solomon were considered even more sacred. Even when Herod rebuilt the second Temple, the use of gold on the many gates was lavish.

The main outer gate of this Temple was the costliest one, since it was made entirely of brass. It was called, in fact, "the Beautiful Gate." It was at this gate that St. Peter cured the lame man. "Silver and gold I do not have but what I have I give you: In the name of Jesus of Nazareth, rise and walk" (Acts 3:1-10).

I stood in awe before the gates of St. Peter's Basilica in Rome. Michelangelo said of Ghiberti's gates to the baptistry in Florence that they were worthy to be gates for Paradise. No doubt at all but that the beauty of Mary's soul enters into the use of this title for her.

The poetry and imagery of gates also impressed the Psalmist greatly. We have "Lift up, O gates, your lintels, reach up you ancient portals, that the king of glory may come in" (Ps 24:7), and "Enter his gates with thanksgiving, his courts with praise" (100:4), as well as "Open to me the gates of justice; I will enter them and give thanks to the Lord. This is the Lord's own gate; the just shall enter it" (118:19-20).

Surely it is easy to see how these and like verses from the Psalter can be applied to Mary. She is the Gate through whom the King of Glory entered into the world. Mary leads us before the throne of justice with songs of thanksgiving for the peace and reconciliation that Christ has won for us. St. John's description of the new Jerusalem in the Book of Revelation dwells lovingly on the beauty of its gates which we have as a popular expression, "the pearly gates of Heaven" (21:21). Christian devotion easily applied this to Mary, the New Eve, the First Lady of the heavenly city.

One of the prophecies that attracted the saintly authors as an applied Marian text, is from Ezeckiel 43:4, and 44:2-3. The glory of the Lord left the Temple through the East Gate, and it was then to be forever closed so that no human could use it.

St. Jerome writes in his *Commentary on Ezekiel*, "This gate shall be closed, says the prophet, and it will not be opened. Beautiful indeed is that closed gate through which only the Lord God of Israel may enter, the Leader for whom it has been closed.

"The Blessed Virgin Mary is that beautiful closed gate. She was a virgin before childbirth and she remained a virgin after childbirth. . . . Forever Mary is a Virgin."

And St. Aelred of Riveaux adds, "The most holy Mary is this Eastern Gate. For a gate which looks toward the East is the first to reflect the rays of the sun. So, the most blessed Mary . . . received the first rays of the sun, or rather the whole blaze of light of that true sun. This gate was shut and well guarded. The enemy could find no entrance whatever."

So, under many signs and symbols, Mary is for us the Gate of Heaven. When we return home to her in Heaven, we pray that she will be waiting for us at the gate to welcome us and lead us to her Son.

35

Morning Star

There is a fascination about astronomers that can hardly be disguised, since these scientists are wrestling with the vast reaches of God's universe and trying to give us new insights into the very act of Divine Creation.

They deal in light years and galaxies and star systems and novas and the like. If men do not destroy our planet with nuclear weapons or worse, the astronomers are charting the future expansion of the human race, until God tells time to cease.

But the romantic and the poets have a much greater joy in the stars than do all the physical scientists. The stars of night illuminate the time of love and mystery. The morning star precedes the dawn and is a herald of the full sunlight of daytime.

Was ever an imagery made to describe the Blessed Mother with more loving care?

She is the morning star who heralds and brings the true Son of Justice into the world. Before He who is Light from Light could illuminate the world, Mary was chosen to be His route into the world. From her the Son of Justice brought the daylight of God's glory to the world of mankind.

"Who is she," sings the Church, "that comes forth like the dawn, as beautiful as the moon, as resplendent as the sun, as awe-inspiring as bannered troops?" (Sg 6:10D).

St. Bernard, who wrote while men still thought the earth was flat, could take off into flights of spiritual ecstasy with this notion of Mary as Star:

"She is most beautifully likened to a star," he says, "for a star pours forth its light without losing anything of its nature. She gave us her Son without losing anything of her virginity. The glowing rays of a star take nothing away from its beauty. Neither has the Son taken anything away from his Mother's integrity."

Then Bernard refers to the famous oracle of the false prophet Balaam, "A star shall advance from Jacob ..." (Nm 24:17) and writes, "She is that noble star of Jacob, illuminating the whole world, penetrating from the highest heavens to the deepest depths of hell. The warmth of her brilliance shines in the minds of men, encouraging virtue, extinguishing vice.

"She is that glorious star lighting the way across the vast ocean of life, glowing with merits, guiding by example."

The Star of Bethlehem also figures prominently in the life of Mary. Those mysterious men from the second chapter of St. Matthew's Gospel, the Magi, more astrologers than scientists, claimed that they had seen Christ's star rising.

What did they see? We'll never really know this side of Judgment Day. Was it some configuration in the heavens that they interpreted according to their arcane rites? Was it a miracle which only they saw? From the way they describe it, it did not act like any star that we have ever heard of before, or since. How could it have pointed out one little spot in Bethlemen? No doubt it was a miraculous occurrence given to them to bring them on their journey. God so often uses the things with which we are familiar to lead us into the unknown country of faith.

That didn't bother the saints, who loved to comment in much the manner St. Leo did: "Still, the heavens themselves declared the glory of God and the news of this truth spread.

"The angelic host announced the birth of the Savior to the shepherds. The star brought the Magi to adore him, that the birth of the Lord might shine forth from the rising of the sun until its setting, that the kingdoms of the East might learn from the Magi the great truths of faith that would spread through the Roman Empire."

St. John Chrysostom gives us a spiritual interpretation of the Magi's visit: "They saw him not as a mere human being but as God, their Benefactor. They were in no way deceived by externals, so they adored him and gave gifts. This is so very direct. . .

"The Magi did not sacrifice sheep and calves. They offered gifts which Christians might imitate: knowledge, obedience and love."

The six-pointed Star of David, which Mary knew and loved so well, has been supplanted by the five-pointed Star of Bethlehem, which has become a symbol of the Nativity and of all the love that Jesus and Mary have for us. How many billions of Christmas cards have given a place of prominence to "the Star"!

Another star image that Christians have always loved and attributed to the Blessed Mother is taken from St. John's vision recorded in the twelfth chapter of the Book of Revelation. "A great sign appeared in the sky, a woman clothed with the sun, with the moon under her feet, and on her head a crown of twelve stars."

"This woman," says St. Augustine, "is the Virgin Mary who, preserving her own virginal integrity, gave birth to the Virgin Head of the Church. In this, Mary symbolizes the Church. She, a virgin, brought forth her Son. Holy Mother Church, herself a virgin, constantly brings forth children, also remaining a virgin."

The image of Mary as Star of the Sea has brought forth some of the finest of Christian art and literature. St. Bonaventure compares life to a tempestuous sea into which sinners have fallen from the ship of divine grace. He pictures Our Lord saying to them, "O poor lost sinners, despair not; raise up your eyes and look at this beautiful star."

St. Ephrem calls her "the safe harbor of all sailing on the sea of the world."

St. Thomas Aquinas observes that "as sailors steer their ship to port by watching the stars, so Christians are brought to glory by the intercession of Mary."

St. Bernard has written the classic meditation on Mary as Star of the Sea in the second of his *Missus Est* homilies:

"When you find yourself tossed by the raging storms of this great sea of life, far from land, keep your eyes fixed on this Star to avoid disaster. When the winds of temptation or the rocks of tribulation threaten, look up to the Star, call upon Mary!

"When the waves of pride or ambition sweep over you, when the tide of detraction or jealously runs against you, look up to the Star, call upon Mary! When the shipwreck of avarice, anger or lust seems imminent, call upon Mary!"

And he concludes: "In the scintillating light of this Star our fervent service of her Son will glow ever more brilliant."

St. Germanus reminds us that "devotion to Mary is a sign either that the soul is already in the state of grace or that it will very soon be so." That is why the Church constantly encourages us to grow in devotion to her. As St. Francis de Sales points out, "Perfection is never finished. We must always be willing to begin again." We can always grow and advance in our love for Mary.

It is hard to conceive of an established Catholic church that does not have a statue or picture of the Blessed Mother. In many countries, outdoor shrines to her dot the countryside. The picture of Our Lady of Guadalupe predominates in Hispanic areas. Every Catholic nation has its own special devotion to Mary.

How true, then, that Mary is the Morning Star who precedes and encourages love and devotion to Jesus Christ.

Stella matutina, ora pro nobis!

36

Health of the Sick

In the old Basilica of Our Lady of Guadalupe, the rule for celebrating Mass at the main altar where "the" picture was enshrined was that it was reserved for bishops and newly-ordained Mexican priests. Since my Spanish was not very good, I missed the stress on Mexican and vested and proceeded to offer one of my "very early" Masses at the altar.

However, the thing that amazed me most, after gazing in awe at the picture, was the number of votive offerings that surrounded the shrine and spilled over into chapels and sacristies. They were a vivid testimony to the huge number of cures that have been granted to pilgrims to this venerable shrine.

The ancient English have a saying to the effect that a saint who grants few miracles will have few pilgrims. If that is true, then so must be the reverse, because pilgrims continue to visit Guadalupe in droves.

The same is repeated at Marian shrines around the world such as Lourdes, Fatima, and Knock. Mary as "Health of the Sick" is a literal devotion that springs up naturally in Christian hearts.

Mary is loved as the patroness who is interested in our physical health, our spiritual health, and our happy death. As proof of that just consider the number of Catholic hospitals around the world dedicated to the Blessed Mother. I would hate to have to try to count just the number of hospitals dedicated to Our Lady of Mercy, or just simply Mercy Hospitals.

The spiritual and corporal works of mercy have long been accepted as a proof of our living faith, a faith that comes alive through charity. They can certainly be traced right back to the example and words of Our Lord, such as the beatitudes (Mt 5:3-11; Lk 6:20-26).

Christ even left a special sacrament, the Anointing of the Sick, for those in need. It is meant to restore spiritual health, and if for the spiritual good involved, also physical health (Jas 5:13-15).

St. Polycarp, who died about the year A.D. 110, wrote: "Priests should be sympathetic and merciful to everyone, bringing back those who have wandered, visiting the sick and the poor. Deacons, in the same way, must be blameless in the sight of God.

"Be steadfast, then, and follow the Lord's example, strong and unshaken in faith, loving the community as you love one another. United in the truth, show the Lord's own gentleness in your dealings with one another, and look down on no one. If you can do good, do not put it off, because almsgiving frees one from death."

Christian devotion spontaneously sees in Mary the prime candidate for following the example of her Son in loving works of mercy. As has been pointed out frequently, Mary could not have been a stranger to sickness and deathbeds in her own lifetime.

Tradition has it that Mary was the child of the old age of St. Ann and St. Joachim, and artists have often depicted her as caring for her aged parents and assisting at their deathbed.

St. Joseph, who figures so strongly in the Infancy Narratives, is missing from the Public Life of Christ, and, indeed, the way Christ is referred to indicates that Mary was a widow at that time.

Christian devotion has made St. Joseph the patron saint of a happy death because he was assisted in his last hours and moments with the presence of Jesus and Mary. Speaking of the respect due St. Joseph, Pope Benedict XV writes, "By St. Joseph we are led directly to Mary, and by Mary to the fountain of all holiness, Jesus Christ, who sanctified the domestic virtues by his obedience to St. Joseph and Mary."

Mary's place in the history of Christ's own passion

and death help us realize how intimately Mary knew the grief of the sick and the dying. She united her own martyrdom along with her Son, as He offered Himself to the Father for us.

Important as it is that we can turn to Mary for help and comfort in sickness and trials, she is even more important to us in the promotion and defense of our spiritual health.

Pope Innocent III writes, "Whoever is in the night of sin should cast his eyes on the moon, that is, implore Mary for help, since she reflects the Son of Justice and mercy." She will certainly give him light to see the misery of his state and the strength to leave it without delay.

St. Methodious adds that "by the prayers of Mary almost innumerable sinners are converted."

In Hawaii, there is a beautiful site called the City, or Place, of Refuge. Criminals who made it safely there were protected. In ancient Judea there were designated cities of refuge which also offered protection. St. John Damascene says, in Mary's name, "I am the city of refuge to all who come to me."

For all the miraculous cures at Lourdes there are also countless numbers of people who leave without the physical cure. However, the statement has been made many times that the inner healing and peace of mind that occur are frequently of more importance than the outward cure. To see suffering and pain for the purifying element involved is a great grace. To be able to unite it with the suffering and death of Christ is even more meritorious.

For even those who are cured, death will result from some other set of circumstances. And, as St. Thomas More writes, "How many men attain health of body who would be better off, for their soul's health, if they were still ill?"

Death is inevitable and if Mary can help us come to terms with that, and assist us at the hour of our death, then we have received an even greater blessing.

Father Damien, the leper, is honored by the world because he gave his life to help the lepers on Molokai and to ease their pain and death. However, it was zeal for souls that motivated Damien and makes him a hero in our eyes. St. Elizabeth Ann Seton told her followers, "Love the sick for they are the blessings of the community."

St. Alphonsus writes movingly on the agonies of the dying and the efforts of the powers of hell to grasp the soul at that last moment. More powerful still is the intercession of the Blessed Mother for those in their agony.

St. Alphonsus pictures her as coming, with all her powerful assistance and with all the help she wants from the heavenly cohorts, to defend the souls of her clients, and of all who turn to her Son for mercy. The Blessed Mother assured St. Bridget of this, for speaking of her devout followers at the point of death she said, "Then will I, their dear Lady and Mother, fly to them that they may have consolation and comfort."

Those of us who have been born Catholics and have been devoted to the Rosary — how many millions of times have we concluded that most beautiful of Marian prayers with the petition:

". . . Holy Mary, Mother of God, pray for us sinners, now and at the hour of our death. Amen."

Baroque Madonna and Child in the Bernini style

37

Refuge of Sinners

Leprosy is a dread disease because it is a sort of living death. Slowly the body is eaten away until some major organ is attacked and death follows. Modern medicine can halt the disease, but it cannot cure it. Now we call it by a scientific name, but we continue to isolate the victims.

A pilgrimage to Father Damien's work on the peninsula that juts out from the cliffs of Molokai is a soul-enriching journey in every way. When you see the conditions under which he worked, when you understand the plight of the victims, and when you begin to realize what went on in his soul the morning he began his Sunday homily with the words, "We lepers . . ." then you begin to understand what goes into making a hero for God.

We spent most of a day with the lepers in the leprosarium, talking with them, visiting them in their work places, and exploring the shrine church and the parish church. We were allowed to share everything with them except we could not visit their well-kept homes or eat and drink with them.

It was then that the words of the saints who speak of sin as the moral equivalent of leprosy began to take on real meaning. We dread this disease because we see how terrible and final it is. We are able to live with our mortal sins because they are invisible. What a tragedy, indeed!

That sin is so tragic can be deduced by the price that God demands. He did not hesitate to send His own Son into the world, and Jesus did not hesitate to lay down His life for all of us. God so loved the world that He sent His only-begotten Son, and the Son so loved us that He gave His life for our salvation.

And when Christ paid the price, it was not with some easy words or deeds. He died the cruel and ignoble death of crucifixion. Every pain that Christ suffered had infinite worth, unlimited merit. The pain of the circumcision would have sufficed, yet Christ willed to go the whole and complete way and show that His love was also infinite.

Mary stood with Christ. As she brought Him into the world, so she offered Him at the end of His Public Life and became, with Him, a willing sacrificial victim for sin.

To call Mary the Refuge of Sinners now has much more meaning. It isn't just her mercy or love that we commemorate. Mary knows the cost of sin, knows as much as any human being can how much her Son loves sinners, and she too longs to gather them in as the fruits of Calvary.

Forget the quaint medieval legends that make Christ the terrible just Judge and Mary the Font of Mercy. They are testimony to the great love the people had for Mary and a testimony to her powerful intercession. However, Mary cooperated in Christ's work and she hates sin just as much as He does, humanly speaking, even though they both love the sinner — obviously!

Because of Christ's sacrificial love, we can approach the throne of God with confidence (Eph 3:11-13). Knowing our own weakness and the fact that we can and do backslide, then having the Mother of God exercise maternal intercession for us is only an additional cause for confidence. It is another instance of Christ's understanding the human heart so well and adapting to our weakness.

Our Lord assured the Apostles that they would stand on twelve thrones judging the twelve tribes of Israel. It's a beautiful symbolism of their importance in the work He decreed, the foundation of the Church, but it is strictly in our own best interests that Jesus, the God-man, will be our just and loving Judge. We cannot do better than trust ourselves to the Sacred Heart of Jesus!

With this clearly understood, then Mary's title the Refuge of Sinners takes on the beauty that God wishes it to have. When we are bowed down with the enormity of our sins, when despair seems the only answer, then the maternal love of the Blessed Mother gives us that extra human courage to go, with her, into the presence of her Son.

One day I was called to a nearby prison to talk with a Hispanic prisoner who was being especially difficult and who was accused of an especially heinous crime. I have no expertise as a prison chaplain, then or now, but all the knowledgeable priests were off on retreat, so I was called.

I was doing a thoroughly incompetent job and I was at my wit's end. Finally, as a truly last resort, I said, "Well, I have said Mass before the image of the Virgin of Guadalupe in Mexico City." To my astonishment, he burst into tears, buried his head on my shoulder and began to sob out his story. We were finally able to get some help for him.

That's why the Place of Refuge on the big island of Hawaii makes such an impression. We need every human help we can get when remorse and repentance come over us and we want to do better. We need all the help we can get.

The cities of refuge in the Old Testament and the right of sanctuary in medieval Europe are in this same league. King Ine of Wessex, in the late seventh century seems to have been one of the first to grant the right of sanctuary in writing, and a century or so later it is found in the decrees of the Council of Mainz. These were repeated by King Alfred the Great and King Edward the Confessor, echoing laws that were established in continental Europe much earlier.

Father Junipero Serra founded his Missions in California as places where the Indian converts could be preserved from the bad habits and bad example of European Christians and could safely grow in their faith. This has been the experience of missionaries before and after him, that a safe refuge is needed for the new Christians before they are mature enough to take their place in the world.

After these examples, then, Mary is referred to by the saints as a place of refuge, of safe asylum, of sanctuary. St. John of Damascus thus proclaimed that Mary is not only the refuge of the innocent, but also for the wicked who implore her protection. He calls her "a city of refuge for all who turn to her."

St. Bonaventure remarks that Mary embraces with maternal love even such a sinner as is despised by all the world, and doesn't stop embracing him until he is reconciled with his Judge. St. Germanus adds, "She is the ever-ready refuge of sinners."

Speaking of her all-powerful intercession, St. Bernard says very firmly, "O Mother of God, you do not disdain a sinner no matter how loathsome he may be; if he sends up his sighs to you, you will deliver him from despair with your own hand."

The Christian virtue of hope makes life livable. Since Jesus has given us His Mother, the Refuge of Sinners, to be "Our life, our sweetness, and our hope," as we proclaim so eloquently in the hymn *Salve Regina*, we have all this additional confidence that, as we repent from our sins, we may again find great favor with God and the courage to begin again to make great progress in becoming more Christlike.

38

Comforter of the Afflicted
(Comfort of the Troubled)
(Consoler of the Afflicted)

Granting the human condition, and without quibbling about the nature or definition of Original Sin, we live in a "vale of tears" as the *Salve Regina* describes it so well.

The technocrats keep improving the quality of life for those who can afford it, yet the stress and strain of modern living takes an inevitable toll. As fast as the medical profession conquers one dread disease, another comes along, such as AIDS.

As the virtue of penance, with its fasting and self-denial, loses popularity, the indulgence of human nature leads to less and less happiness. If we cannot learn to say "No" to ourselves in things we can have, how can we say "No" to ourselves in things we cannot have?

Whatever our answers, we live amid afflictions and troubles, and we turn to Mary, the Comforter of the Afflicted, for her powerful maternal help. She can be sympathetic since she knows what the human condition is. She has experienced it. St. Alphonsus Liguori gives a whole section in *The Glories of Mary* to the "Dolors of Mary." Her seven sorrows have prepared her, by experience, to be ready to help us in our time of sorrow.

Perhaps the most beautiful treatment of Mary's own sorrows is in the sequence *Stabat Mater*. This moving poem is attributed to the thirteenth-century Franciscan Jacopone da Todi. In a simpler form it goes back at least another century.

At the cross her station keeping,
Stood the mournful Mother weeping,

Close to Jesus to the last.
Through her heart, His sorrow sharing,
All His bitter anguish bearing,
Now at length the sword has pierced (v.1)

The prophecy of Simeon had now come to pass. This
sorrow had been with Mary ever since the time of the
Presentation. No doubt before that, during her three-
month Visitation with Elizabeth, these two prophetesses had discussed the fulfillment of the prophecies of
which they were now a part. They must have mused
over the idea of the Suffering Servant of Yahweh.

Now Mary was a faithful witness, a participant, "all
His bitter anguish sharing." Her Immaculate Heart
was purified through her will to unite herself to the bitter agonies of His Sacred Heart.

Bruised, derided, cursed, defiled,
She beheld her tender Child
All with bloody scourges rent;
For the sins of His own nation,
Saw Him hang in desolation
Till His Spirit forth He sent (v.4)

The scourging at the pillar was a torture so severe
that Christ usually referred to "the scourging and
crucifixion" together. The only pain He had suffered
previously was at the Circumcision. Now He seemed to
dread the scourging with particular concern. Mary's
witness to this, in the broken, bloody, bruised body on
the cross, was an excruciating element of her own suffering.

The Church applies to her the words at the beginning of the Lamentations, "O all you who pass by the
way, look and see if there is any sorrow like my sorrow!" Beyond any doubt, Mary learned to comfort
others by what she suffered.

That is what St. Ephrem means when he titles her

"the comfort of the world, the mother of orphans, the liberator of prisoners, and the redeemer of captives."

St. Germanus asks, "O Mary, who, after your own Son, is as solicitous for the whole human race as you are? Who protects us in our trials as you do?" St. Antoninus replies, "No saint can be found who compassionates us in our miseries as does this most loving Lady, the Blessed Virgin Mary."

The miseries that afflict us are troubles in body, mind, and soul. Blessed Henry Suso calls Mary "the most faithful comfortress of sinners." St. Alphonsus Liguori adds, "We need only show Mary the wounds of our souls and she immediately helps us by her prayers, and consoles us."

Variations of this title are "Our Lady of Pity," "Our Lady of the Forsaken," and "Our Lady of Mercy." This is probably the most familiar to us, and it is reflected in many shrines to Our Lady under that title. In fact, these four titles in the Litany, Health of the Sick, Refuge of Sinners, Consoler of the Afflicted and Help of Christians, are grouped together by Father Albert Power as "the Mercy Titles."

The story of St. Jerome Emiliani is typical. He was a Venetian nobleman and a brave soldier, with the usual habits prevalent among the military. While in prison after a defeat, he determined to change his sinful life, and he turned to Mary to beg the courage and strength he would need.

She responded with his freedom, and he gave the rest of his life in the service of orphan children. Mary had comforted him in his darkest hour, and he spent the rest of his life helping and comforting his young, homeless wards.

Mary also has a very tender love for the Souls in Purgatory. The "Great Promise" of the brown (Carmelite) scapular is that on the Saturday following the death of a person wearing this emblem, she will come and release them from Purgatory if they are there.

St. Bernardine of Siena says that "in that prison (Purgatory), where souls that are espoused to Jesus Christ are detained, Mary has a certain dominion and plenitude of power, not only to relieve them, but even to deliver them."

"How courteous and benign," says St. Vincent Ferrer, "is the most Blessed Virgin to those who suffer in Purgatory! Through her they constantly receive comfort and refreshment."

Many of the saints looked at the great feasts of the Blessed Mother as a special time of grace for the souls in Purgatory. What greater tribute to her than that she would lead countless souls to her Son's court to celebrate her triumphs. It is very logical in the light of our human devotion.

The Blessed Mother sent this message to the Cistercian sacristan Blessed Godfrey (Geoffrey), "Try to advance rapidly in virtue so that you will belong to my Son and to me. Then when your soul departs, I will not let it go to Purgatory but will take it and offer it to my Son."

If there seems to be no end to the comfort and consolation that Mary extends to those in need or in trouble, I would have to agree. These people, living and dead, are precious members of her Son's body, the Church; they are special sons and daughters of God, reborn in Baptism to the life of Christ; and she is the Mother.

If she does not remove the affliction, she obtains for us the grace to bear it patiently and with spiritual profit. That may be an even better answer, that we learn conformity to the will of God and the virtue of patience.

In a hymn that is over a thousand years old, the *Ave Maris Stella*, we pray "Break the sinners' fetters, restore light to the blind, dispel all our ills, and ask for us all that is good."

St. Alphonsus Liguori composed this little prayer to

Mary, Comfortress of the Afflicted. "O Mary, console us always but especially at the hour of our death; come at that last hour and receive our souls and present them yourself to your Son, who will judge us."

39
Help of Christians

There is no Marian tradition older than that expressed in the powerful title, "Mary Help of Christians." The oldest known prayer to the Blessed Virgin was found on a Greek papyrus dating from the end of the third century. It is known by its Latin title, *Sub Tuum*:

"We turn to you for protection,
Holy Mother of God.
Listen to our prayers
And help us in our needs.
Save us from every danger,
Glorious and blessed Virgin."

There are interesting variations of this title under which Our Lady is venerated. They include Our Lady of Prompt Succor, Our Lady of Perpetual Help, and Notre Dame de Bon Secours.

The credit for adding the title Help of Christians to the Litany of Loreto goes to Pope St. Pius V in 1571. This was the occasion:

The Moslems had been making signal military gains throughout the Eastern Mediterranean, and finally they captured Lepanto, not far from the Italian peninsula.

The city-state of Venice formed a coalition with Spain, Genoa, and the Papal States to block the Moslem navy. An armada of galleys went forth to meet the Moslem galleys. This was the last great naval battle fought with rowed boats. The Christian fleet cornered the Moslems off the coast of Lepanto, and though vastly outnumbered, inflicted a great defeat on them.

The pope, meanwhile, had ordered Masses and Rosaries to beg God's favor on this vast undertaking, so necessary to preserve Christianity in Europe. It has been reported that the pope himself offered five Masses on the day of battle, September 7, 1571.

When news of the victory reached Rome, the pope instituted the Feast of the Holy Rosary for September 7, as an annual feast of thanksgiving, and he ordered the inclusion of the title Help of Christians in the Litany.

It was another century before the Moslems were able to mount another major threat to Europe, and this was overland, and directed at Vienna. The military genius Sobieski led the Christians to victory, but not before he was seen at Mass, arms outstretched in the form of the cross, receiving Holy Communion and imploring the powerful intercession of the Mother of God.

The actual Feast of Our Lady, Help of Christians, was instituted by Pope Pius VII. He suffered greatly at the hands of Napoleon Bonaparte, including exile and virtual imprisonment. In his arrogance Napoleon believed that he had the power to destroy the Church. When he made this boast to the Cardinal Secretary of State, that prelate responded with the shake of his head, "No, sire, in eighteen hundred years not even the priests have been able to do that." However apocryphal that story may be, it reflects the Emperor's mind.

During all these troubles, the pope had encouraged Catholics everywhere to pray the Rosary for the freedom of the Church. When Pope Pius VII was finally released at the time of Napoleon's abdication, he instituted the Feast of Mary, Help of Christians to be commemorated on May 24, the day of his first release from exile.

Ann Ball, in *A Litany of Mary*, which details forty famous Marian shrines, mentions an old Bavarian shrine which had a picture of Mary under this title. She says, "Pilgrims to this shrine prayed the short prayer, 'Maria, hilf!'" How beautifully direct — Mary, help!

A more familiar picture is the one we know as Our

Lady of Perpetual Help. While some maintain that it represents a traditional likeness going back to St. Luke himself, the more probable explanation is that it comes from the thirteenth century.

It shows the Madonna and Child in a typical Byzantine iconographic form, with Archangels Michael and Gabriel on either side, showing the instruments of the Passion.

It arrived in Rome from Crete near the end of the fifteenth century, where it was honored by great crowds until the French, under Napoleon, entered Rome in 1812 and destroyed the Church of St. Matthew, which housed the picture.

Forty years later it was rediscovered in an Augustinian chapel where it had been placed to save it. Pope Pius IX, who had prayed before it as a boy, gave it to the Redemptorists at the Church of St. Alphonsus, and they, with papal approbation, have spread the devotion throughout the Christian world.

Montreal recognizes Notre Dame de Bon Secours as the one whose intercession saved the city from a grave epidemic. In New Orleans, the Ursuline Nuns honor a statue of Our Lady of Prompt Succor, and during the Battle of New Orleans in 1815 they kept constant vigil before it for the American forces.

After General Jackson won the battle, he and his staff visited the convent to thank the nuns for their prayers. Every year since then, a Mass of thanksgiving has been celebrated.

One of the most zealous clients of Our Lady under her title Help of Christians has been St. John Bosco. He was certainly an unlikely founder of a great religious congregation, one which began so humbly. He and his mother responded to the needs of some homeless street boys, took them in, put them under the patronage of Mary, and the work took off.

Don Bosco turned to the moderate spirituality of St. Francis de Sales for his rule, and the modern Salesians are now a worldwide congregation, dedicated to the various practical works of the Christian social apostolate and still running schools and homes for boys.

In his personal spiritual life, St. John Bosco turned constantly and consistently to Mary, Help of Christians, in all his needs. In gratitude for her outstanding intercession in his behalf and the many favors he received from her, he started the last basilica to go up in Rome, dedicated, of course, to Mary, Help of Christians.

I have celebrated Mass in this basilica, and while it is far from finished, it is usable and impressive. And anyway, who expects a basilica to be finished in only a century?

It can be seen that Mary's help extends to the Church and the pope, to the cause of freedom and human dignity, and indeed, into the lives of all who seek her. St. Bernard says to Mary, "You are an invincible warrior in defense of your servants, fighting against the devils who assail them."

St. John Damascene salutes Mary as "the prepared and always ready help of Christians, by which they are delivered from dangers." St. Thomas Aquinas remarks that he had never asked anything from God through the intercession of Mary without obtaining it, or something better.

The Antiphon formerly used at Vespers for Feasts of Our Lady expresses it so beautifully:

"Holy Mary,
Help those in need,
Give strength to the weak,
Comfort the sorrowful,
Pray for God's people,
Assist the clergy,
Intercede for religious.
May all who seek your help
experience your unfailing protection."

40
Queen of Angels

St. Peter Canisius, the brilliant Jesuit theologian, proclaims the devout belief of Catholics in this way. "Why did the Fathers of the Church call the Virgin Mary by the title 'Queen'? They recognized the tremendous praise heaped on her in the Scriptures.

"She is signaled out as having a King for her father, the noble David, and the King of Kings and Lord of Lords for her Son, whose reign will never end. . . .

"There is not one who excels her in dignity, beauty or holiness. Only the Holy Trinity is above her; all others are below her in dignity and beauty."

Since this is true, Mary's reign extends over all creatures, from the highest to the least. To call her the Queen of the Angels is a logical conclusion, awesome as that title may seem.

The angelic creation could not be deduced from strict reasoning. Their existence is known to us only through Revelation. And throughout the Scriptures, the angelic "messengers," as their name teaches, are seen fulfilling the will of God towards us.

St. Thomas distinguishes three hierarchies of angelic creation, each with three orders. First are the Seraphim, the Cherubim and the Thrones. In second place are the Dominations, the Virtues and the Powers. Finally there are the Principalities, Archangels and Angels. Of all of these, Mary is the Queen.

Notice how often Our Lord was the object of angelic ministrations. It started at the moment of the Incarnation, when Mary answered *fiat* to the archangel St. Gabriel, through the Nativity events when the angelic hosts opened the sky with their chant, "Glory to God in the highest and on earth peace to those on whom his favor rests" (Lk 2:14).

The exile in Egypt was directed by angelic messages. The next public event is Our Lord's temptation, but it seems obvious to many of the saintly writers that the angels were no strangers at Nazareth.

We are not surprised that angels ministered to the Lord at Gethsemane, and we certainly expect the angels of the Resurrection and the Ascension.

St. Thomas Aquinas is of the opinion that St. Gabriel was *the* angel of the Incarnation, and so we can expect that all of these angelic ministrations in Our Lord's stay on earth were performed or led by Gabriel. That angel's greeting to Mary was certainly in accord with the respect he owed his Queen, the Mother of the King whose birth he announced.

St. Bede the Venerable remarks, "It was an apt beginning that man's redemption was announced when an angel approached a Virgin who would bring forth a Divine Son. The beginning of man's ruin was caused when the serpent, sent by the devil, successfully tempted the woman to bring forth the wounds of pride."

To which St. Jerome adds, "How fitting that an angel be sent to the Virgin. Virginity is always close to the angelic life. Certainly to live in the flesh but not for the flesh is more a heavenly life than an earthly one."

The theologian Francis Suarez states it boldly, "With regard to the most excellent Virgin Mary, as the Church herself sings, she is exalted above all the choirs of angels in the heavenly kingdom. It is certain that among all creatures, no matter how pure, the Blessed Virgin exceeds all in beatitude, even the angels. . . . She alone is superior to all creatures in essential beatitude."

Further on in his *Treatise on the Angels* he says, "Just as Christ is the Head of the angels, Mary is their Queen and Mistress. In their grades and orders they are also her servants. Just as they always contemplate the Word, they always venerate and love her."

Knowing how frail mankind is in the face of temptation, Divine Providence has provided each and every one of us with a Guardian Angel (cf. Mt 18:10). It is the thinking of many scholars that groups, churches, nations, and the rest also have their Guardian Angels. The poet opined, "Touch but a stone and turn an angel's wing!"

And Mary is Queen of all of these angels, too.

"The tremendous thought," writes Father Hugh Blunt, "is that Mary is Queen of Angels, that she, who by nature is inferior to them, is in dignity superior to them, due to the fact that she has the supreme dignity, that of Mother of God."

Speaking of Mary's Assumption into Heaven, St. Anselm declares, "And now Mary herself is exalted above the choirs of Angels; now all her desire is fulfilled, she sees God face to face, as He is, and rejoices with her Son forever."

Devotion to St. Michael is also linked to Mary. The Church frequently applies the passages in the Book of Revelation, on the Woman crowned with the stars, to the Blessed Mother. There the Woman is defended by St. Michael and his legions (Rv 12). As the Holy Family traversed the dangerous path to Egypt, as the enemies of Jesus surrounded Him on all sides, it is devoutly held that St. Michael was always present as defender and protector.

At the end of the sixth century, when a plague attacked the city of Rome, Pope St. Gregory the Great led a procession of the people from the Church of Ara Coeli to St. Peter's. As they passed the tomb of Hadrian, voices were heard chanting the *Regina Coeli* and an angel was seen sheathing his sword. The name of the castle tomb was changed to that of the Holy Angel Michael, or Sant'angelo.

In his role as defender and protector, St. Michael is considered a special patron of the dying, so that, as the devils contend for their souls at that great moment of crisis, St. Michael is there to protect and guide the soul into heaven. Therefore, many believe St. Michael told the Blessed Mother when her life was to end, and escorted her along with a retinue of angels into Heaven.

These pious conclusions are tenable, especially when we consider the great dignity and power that are the prerogative of the Queen of Angels. We salute her in the fifteenth mystery of the Rosary as the crowned Queen of Heaven and Earth.

Modern popes frequently refer to the Blessed Mother as "exalted above all the choirs of angels," and "Queen and sovereign of angels." Pope Pius XII used these and similar terms at least six times.

The Second Vatican Council, near the end of its important document *Lumen Gentium*, the Dogmatic Constitution on the Church, clearly indicates Mary's supremacy four times, including: "As the most holy Mother of God she was exalted by divine grace above all angels and men" (60). We can rejoice in this and the rest of the queenly titles as they indicate Mary's importance in the economy of salvation and in the hierarchy of Christian devotional affairs. It is our joy to honor her, following the example of her Son.

It also means, moreover, that this powerful Mother has, at her command, whatever we, her devout clients, need. Because she is the Queen Mother of Heaven, she can help us; because she is our Mother too, she will help us. How great, then, is our motivation to join with the choirs of angels in singing her praises:

Hail, O Queen of heaven enthroned!
Hail, by Angels Mistress owned!
Root of Jesse, Gate of morn,
Whence the world's true Light is born:
Glorious Virgin, joy to thee,
Loveliest whom in heaven we see:
Fairest thou where all are fair,
Plead with Christ our sins to spare.
Ave Regina coelorum (Father Edward Caswell)

41

Queen of Patriarchs
Queen of Prophets
Queen of Patriarchs
and Prophets

It is curious, indeed, that the reworking of the Litany of Loreto in its latest form, as published in *Book of Mary*, approved by the Bishops' Committee on the Liturgy NCCB/USCC, 23 March 1987, makes a combination of these two significant Marian titles, as well as the next four. There must be a reason, but it completely escapes me.

Queen of Patriarchs

In 1988, Our Sunday Visitor Publishing Division published my book, *Prophecies Fulfilled*. It is a devotional treatment of the Canticles in Luke's Infancy Narrative.

When we look at the *Magnificat*, the *Benedictus*, and to a lesser extent the *Nunc Dimittis*, Mary's consciousness of and pride in her Jewish origins is unmistakable.

At the head of those origins were the Patriarchs Abraham, Isaac, and Jacob. The twelve sons of Jacob (Israel) are patriarchs, the founders of the twelve tribes of Israel. While Moses deserves a place with these great men, he is usually set into his own special category of Lawgiver.

By the time of King David, who is also referred to as a Patriarch, the extended family system of blood relationships and marital relationships is more refined and the word "Patriarchal" already has its modern meaning: the man as founding father and ruler of his family.

The Italians, Spanish, Mexicans, and others in the Western world still have this veneration of the oldest ruling male, although the lines are becoming quite blurred in the English-speaking world. Probably the Irish "tribal" tradition is the only one really left. As we were taught, "Blood is thicker than water." This is being replaced by "You can pick your friends; your relatives are wished on you!"

Mary concludes her great song of praise with the words, "Even as He promised our fathers, promised to Abraham and his seed forever" (Lk 1:55). Mary's pride in her ancestors tells us much about her, and Abraham's history offers much light on the Incarnation.

He left his home and went to Canaan, which became the Jewish homeland, as promised by oath. His subsequent flight into Egypt reminds us of the Holy Family's sojourn there. His tribute to Melchizedek, the King of Salem (Peace), would be a major point in the New Testament writer's description of the priesthood of Christ (Heb 5-7).

God told him that his descendents would be as countless as the stars of heaven (Gn 15:5), but Mary goes beyond this with, "All generations shall call me blessed" (Lk 1:47). Abraham entertains God and two angels, and a son of promise is born miraculously. Gabriel visits Mary, and the Son of God is conceived, miraculously.

On the eighth day, the boy is circumcised and named Isaac. On the eighth day, the Child is circumcised and named Jesus, for He will save His people from their sins (Lk 2:21). Abraham's only-begotten son is demanded by God in sacrifice, and saved only at the last minute. With Mary, the only-begotten Son was not spared.

Abraham is saluted as our "Father in faith" because

of his example of belief and trust in God, but Mary was the first Christian, the first to believe in Jesus Christ.

The Gospels are careful to trace Mary's lineage back to Abraham, and both Mary and Zachariah speak of God's promises to the patriarchs, which Zachariah calls an oath (Lk 1:70,73). At the Presentation, Simeon exults that he is ready to die in peace, because God has fulfilled the word given to the fathers.

How familiar Jesus and Mary were with these promises, repeated over and over in the Temple and synagogue worship. This formed their spirituality, so much so that St. Jerome could say, "Ignorance of the Old Testament is ignorance of Christ."

In like manner, Isaac, the gentle man, and Jacob (Israel) and his twelve sons are types that can be applied directly to Christ and indirectly to Mary. The richness of this patriarchal heritage is almost limitless in application.

St. Bernard alludes to this when he writes, "The circumcision proves, beyond a shadow of doubt, the fact of his humanity; the Name indicates the majesty of his glory. He was circumcised because he was truly a son of Abraham; He was called Jesus, the name that is above all names, because he was truly the Son of God." About the holy Name, Bernard exclaims, "Jesus to me is honey in the mouth, music to the ear, a song in the heart!"

Novatian states, "Therefore let those who read in the scripture that the man Christ Jesus is the Son of Man, also read there that this same Jesus is called both God and the Son of God. In the same manner that he, as man, is of Abraham, even so, as God, is he also before Abraham himself. In the same manner that he, as man, is the Son of David so he is also, as God, called the Lord of David."

Peter Bloisius, in a famous sermon to the priests teaches that, "A priest has the primacy of Abel, the patriarchate of Abraham, the government of Noah, the order of Melchizedek, the dignity of Aaron, the authority of Moses, the perfection of Samuel, the power of Peter, the unction of Christ."

"The divine preparations," as Abbot Columba Marmion, O.S.B. describes them in *Christ in His Mysteries*, includes this passage: "Throughout the years as they pass by, and as the centuries advance, God makes his promise more precise; he repeats it with more solemnity. He assures the Patriarchs, Abraham, Isaac and Jacob, that it is from their race that the blessed seed shall come forth; to the dying Jacob he shows that it is in the tribe of his son Judah that the One who is to come, the desired of the nations, shall arise."

Mary's faith linked her with the promises to the Patriarchs even more than her blood descent. We who have seen the fulfillment of these prophecies and who no longer depend on figures, but who have the fact of Christ, Messiah, rejoice with Mary that Yahweh Himself was faithful to His promises.

Queen of Prophets

One of the most joyful duties of the parish priest is the conferring of the Sacrament of Baptism on infants. Especially if it is a first child, the parents come to church beaming, bursting with pride. Their child will be special and will grow into someone of importance, maybe even President of the United States! The priest can't help but feel something of their joy, and, indeed, feel he is a part of it.

When Mary and Joseph presented the Christ-Child in the Temple, they knew their Child was something special, the long-desired of all the nations, the very Son of God. Did the priest who accepted their "offering of the poor" feel something of their joy? I'll bet he did. It had to be contagious.

Mary was conscious of the fact that she was "the" Woman of promise. When God promised the Savior, the Messiah, after the Original Sin of Adam and Eve, He not only guaranteed that savior, but that the man would be born of a woman. In the Protevangelium we read, "I will put enmity between you and the woman, and between your offspring and hers. He will strike at your head, while you strike at his heel" (Gen 3:15).

Then, through the centuries, however long the actual time, that promise was treasured and handed down. At the time of Jacob (Israel), the promise was made that one of his sons, Judah, would be in the direct line. Finally, to King David, the promise was even more refined, that his offspring would rule forever.

"Because you, O God, have revealed to your servant that you will build him a house. . . and you have deigned to bless the house of your servant so that it will remain forever. . ."(1 Chr 17:25-27).

Mary and Joseph were well aware of these promises: to the seed of Abraham, the tribe of Judah, and the House of David. Then, the prophets, especially Isaiah, Jeremiah, and Daniel, refined the notion of the Messiah and his human condition even more.

Daniel had prophesied the "seventy weeks of years" (9:24), and their fulfillment was due in the lifetime of Mary and Joseph. They were so humble that it never entered their thoughts that they would be so involved with the Messiah. They were just delighted to know that it would happen while they lived.

Did Mary secretly hope that she might be just the servant in the house of the Savior? Is that why her answer came so readily, "Behold the handmaid of the Lord"? Certainly every Jewish woman of the time who had the right lineage must have dreamed and wondered if her son was the One.

Some, like St. Alphonsus Liguori, claim that because of the Immaculate Conception, Mary knew from the very beginning what God had planned for her. In that case, she must have gloried in the fulfillment of the promises as the day drew closer and closer.

St. Tharasius, the Patriarch of Constantinople,

wrote, "You are the mirror of the prophets, the fulfillment of their work. Ezekiel called you the closed gate through which no man has ever passed, save only the Lord God and he kept the gate closed. Isaiah foretold you as the valiant rod of Jesse from which the flower, Christ, would arise to conquer all vice and plant the fields with virtue.

"Jeremiah spoke for God when he said that the days would come in which the Lord would make a new covenant with the house of Israel and the house of Judah, even as he had with their fathers, signifying the advent of your Son who would call all nations to the worship of God. Daniel, that man of great desires, called you the wonderful mountain from which would come the Christ, the cornerstone, to scatter and destroy the works of the serpent."

St. Jerome concurs. "Mary is the glorious eastern gate, says Ezekiel, always closed, concealing in herself, revealing from herself, the Holy of Holies. Through her the Sun of Justice and our High Priest according to the order of Melchisedek, enters and exits at will."

When we salute Mary as Queen of Prophets, we have in mind that she, St. Elizabeth, and St. John the Baptizer were the last of the major Old Testament Prophets, and she was the greatest. Her *Magnificat* contains the highest of the praises of God, particularly because He did fulfill all that He had promised.

Three main ideas dominate that powerful canticle. One, that God's grace has triumphed in her soul; second that he has chosen her from among the "poor of the land" and overlooked the rich and mighty; finally, that all of prophecy is now being fulfilled, summed up in her reference to Abraham.

Mary must have gloried in such prophecies as "Behold, a virgin shall conceive a child and call his name Emmanuel" (Is 7:14), or "The Lord has created a new thing upon the earth. A woman shall compass a Man" (Jer 33:22).

She would have found much fruit in "For a Child is born to us, and a Son is given to us, and the government is upon his shoulder: and, his Name shall be called, Wonderful, Counsellor, God the Mighty, the Father of the world to come, the Prince of Peace" (Is 9:6). (Douay-Rheims translation)

Mary is the Woman of prophecy, from Genesis to the Book of Revelation. She stands portrayed in the Garden of Eden, and she is the Mother of the Church, protecting it against the seductions of the devil until it becomes, in fact, the spotless Bride of Christ at the end of time for all eternity.

Mary remains the prophetess for us in all the many private revelations that have dotted Church history. As at Cana of Galilee, she teaches, "Whatever my Son tells you to do, do!" (Jn 2:1-11). She pleads with us to lead lives of sanctity, to offer our sacrifices and fasting in reparation for sin, to meditate on the mystery of Christ through the Rosary and to become men and women of prayer.

This title Queen of Prophets is not too generally used, but it is so full of meaning that it deserves pondering. All the plans of God for the economy of man's salvation and God's faithfulness to His promises are alluded to in this title. It is truly an awesome title.

42

Queen of Apostles
Queen of Martyrs
Queen of Apostles
and Martyrs

Queen of Apostles

One of the four marks by which the Church of Christ can be recognized is the mark known as apostolic. Christ founded His Church on the Apostles and their successors, and that chain of historic apostolicity is essential to the Church. Without it, a group is simply a pious association of relatively like-minded men and women.

An apostle must have a deep and abiding conviction of the truth of the message he is to deliver, and a real enthusiasm in delivering it. Christ Himself gave the twelve both the message and the mission. Indeed, we might be even more correct in saying He is the message and the mission.

"He who hears you hears me" (Lk 10:16), Christ told them, and "As the Father has sent me, I also send you" (Jn 20:21). At the time of the Ascension He said, "You shall receive power when the Holy Spirit comes upon you, and you shall be witnesses for me in all Judea and Samaria and even to the very ends of the earth" (Acts 1:8).

After the defection of Judas Iscariot, the Apostles brought their number up to twelve again by the selection of St. Matthias. When St. Paul was added to their number by God's direct choice, he gloried in the title Apostle to the Gentiles.

Later on in Church history, many saints would be

given that title for their work in spreading the Faith, such as St. Boniface, Apostle to Germany, or St. Patrick, Apostle to Ireland.

There is a beautiful little church dedicated to the Holy Apostles that I visited in my seminary days. Around the sanctuary were fourteen large niches with thirteen beautiful statues. One niche was left empty. It was very impressive.

As the Apostles began the work of building up the Body of Christ, they had a special reliance on, as well as love of, the Blessed Mother. She earned her title Queen of the Apostles, during her life on earth after Pentecost.

The special relationship between her and St. John is well-known from the words of Christ from the Cross. "Woman, behold your son. . . . Behold, your mother" (Jn 19:26).

However, Mary who brought the Head of the Church into the world was bound to have an essential interest in the members of that Body right from the beginning. How many times the Apostles and first Christians must have turned to her for advice, history, and consolation!

St. Luke tells us that he took great pains and did his research well, to make sure that his Gospel and the Acts were accurate. When you study the first two chapters of his Gospel, he relates things that only a Mother would have known.

These were the things she treasured in her heart and pondered over. These were the words and actions that stayed fully alive in her memory, etched there in vivid pictures.

Her words in the *Magnificat*, Zachary's outpouring of faith and fulfillment in the *Benedictus*, and Simeon's *Nunc Dimittis* were not past history, but ringing echoes in her mind.

Mary had witnessed most of the events of Our Lord's Public Life. His parables were often taken from the most ordinary of home happenings. Didn't he learn these from Mary and Joseph? The parable of the woman looking for the lost coin, the use of leaven in baking, the loving father of the prodigal son, and so on — many of these must have been learned at Nazareth.

St. Anthony of Padua gives us this thought: Jesus wanted His Mother Mary to remain in the world for a certain period of time after His Resurrection so that she might be the Mistress and Guide of the Apostles.

Father James Alberione, S.S.P., in his work, *Mary, Hope of the World*, writes, "When Mary was immersed in a sea of sorrow and love at the foot of the cross on Calvary, Mary's faith did not fail. Stronger than Abraham, she offered her only Son to the Father with the intention of offering everything for the redemption of the world.

"When Jesus was laid in the sepulcher, the Apostles doubted the Resurrection. Mary alone kept the light of faith burning and strengthened the Apostles in this virtue."

The apostolic office continued in the Church through the popes and the bishops. St. Ignatius of Antioch is a striking witness of this in the letters he wrote to the churches as he was a prisoner on the journey to Rome for his martyrdom.

A typical passage is, "All should respect deacons as Jesus Christ, just as all should regard the Bishop as the image of the Father, and the clergy as God's senate and the college of the Apostles. Without these three orders you cannot begin to speak of a Church."

Speaking of the Eucharist, St. Irenaeus observes, "He taught them that this was the new sacrifice of the new covenant. The Church has received this sacrifice from the Apostles." Firmilian adds, "The power of remitting sins was given to the Apostles, and to the churches which they, sent by Christ, established, and to the bishops who succeeded them by vicarious ordination."

Christian piety makes us understand that Mary's love for the Church started with the Apostles and goes down through the centuries of apostolic succession.

This would be particularly true of the missionary activity of the Church. As Queen of the Apostles Mary is certainly Queen of the Missions.

In 1972, the Society for the Propagation of the Faith asked me to write a pamphlet that they could give to benefactors about the founding of that group. The Liturgical Press published it under the title *Charity Without Frontiers.*

It is the story of Marie-Pauline Jaricot who was born in Lyons, France in 1799. Even as a young girl, her heart went out to the poor in her war-ravaged country and to the needs of the missions in China. She devised an ingenious method of "mission circles" through which people would give a penny a week, pool their savings, and help the missions, at home and abroad.

In this way was founded the great work of the Propagation of the Faith. What's its motivation? That Jesus and Mary would be known and loved all over the world.

The mission Christ gave His Apostles lives on, as it will until the end of time. And presiding over our human efforts will be Mary Queen of the Apostles.

Queen of Martyrs

The power and the majesty that are displayed in the Renaissance Madonnas are something to behold. These artists loved to portray the finished product, so to speak, of the Queen Mother now reigning with her Son in Heaven.

But artists have also depicted the martyrdom of Mary as she stood at the foot of the Cross. She who cooperated in making the Incarnation a fact, by that very consent joined herself to His whole work. In Gabriel's joyful greeting was the certitude of Calvary.

Mary is not Queen of Martyrs by courtesy title, but in actual fact. How gladly she would have traded places with Jesus in His Passion and death. If that is the natural maternal instinct in the face of a son's pain, it was multiplied almost infinitely in the Mother of God.

Mary did not physically die a martyr; she died with Christ in spirit and in love. She suffered along with Him, being spared only the agony of that death action. As many of the saints assure us, Mary's martyrdom began as soon as she knew God's plan for her.

"The Passion of Jesus began with his birth," says St. Bernard, and Mary suffered right along with Him. "Mary was a martyr," he adds, "not by the sword of the executioner but by bitter sorrow of heart."

St. Bonaventure points out that "those wounds which were scattered over the whole body of the Lord were all united in the single heart of Mary." St. Ildephonsus sums it up this way. "To say that Mary's sorrows were greater than all the torments of the martyrs united is to say too little."

St. Alphonsus Liguori devotes almost a hundred pages in his work, *The Glories of Mary*, to the Seven Sorrows (Dolors) of Mary. He does this in the context of his devotional treatment of Mary as Queen of Martyrs.

The first sorrow is the prophecy of Simeon at the time of the Presentation of the Lord in the Temple (Lk 2:34-35). In the midst of the joy of that occasion there is the promise of Calvary.

The second sorrow is the Flight into Egypt. The Child is hardly settled in His Mother's arms in Bethlehem when the persecution of Herod began. The wrath and rage of that tyrant were so fierce that, before it was over, the Holy Innocents were slaughtered. The Holy Family certainly suffered all the grief of refugees anywhere in the world.

Next there was the loss of the Child in the Temple in Jerusalem. Most of us consider this in the fifth joyful mystery of the Rosary, emphasizing the sense of recovery, the finding of the Christ Child in the Temple. It's an interesting point to ponder: how close pain and sorrow can be to joy and love.

Mary's fourth sorrow is in her meeting with Jesus on the *Via Dolorosa*. St. Alphonsus describes it this way. "Alas, what a scene of sorrows then presented itself before her! — the nails, the hammers, the cords, the fatal instruments of the death of her Son, all of which were borne before him.

"She raised her eyes and saw, O God! a young man covered with blood and wounds from head to foot. . . . The Mother would have embraced him but the guards thrust her aside with insults. . . . Now where do you go, O Holy Virgin? To Calvary. To Calvary."

The fifth sorrow is the death of Jesus on the Cross. And again, St. Alphonsus: "We have now to witness a new kind of martyrdom — a Mother condemned to see an innocent Son, and one whom she loves with the whole affection of her soul, cruelly tormented and put to death before her own eyes."

The next sorrow is the piercing of the side of Jesus and the descent from the Cross. St. Bernard writes, "The lance which opened his side passed through the soul of the Blessed Virgin, which could never leave her Son's heart." In a most moving way, Fra Angelico captured this sorrow in his *Deposition from the Cross*, as did Michelangelo in the *Pieta*.

The seventh and final sorrow is the burial of Jesus. Even in death His enemies could not leave Him alone. They demanded a guard of Roman soldiers who would guarantee that He stay buried. But that was not to be.

For in all of her martyrdom Mary is also Our Lady of the Resurrection. Through her martyrdom she merited to be the first to receive the presence of the Risen Lord on Easter Sunday. In fact, it is commonly believed that Mary enjoyed His Risen Presence throughout the forty days from Easter to Ascension Thursday.

Because Mary is the Queen of Martyrs, she is the inspiration and comfort of all who have given their lives in witness to Christ. Since the beginning of the Church, the ancient axiom is true: "The blood of martyrs is the seed of Christians."

The early Church marveled at the martyrdom of saints such as Agnes, Cecilia, Agatha, Anastasia, and Lucy. The early successors of St. Peter were all martyrs for the Faith. Mission countries around the world have all had their "proto-martyrs."

For example, when Father Luis Jayme, O.F.M. was put to death by the Indians at Mission San Diego de Alcala in California, Father Junipero Serra rejoiced in his triumphant love, knowing that it was a pledge of God's blessings on the missions.

In our own times, in a Nazi concentration camp, St. Maximilian Kolbe, a true devotee and client of the Mother of God, gave up his life quite directly for the love of God.

It is true, then, as another Christian saying has it, "No cross, no crown." Most of us will never have the grace of martyrdom, or will we? The cross for most of us will come from our fidelity to the duties of our state in life. The triumph of the martyrs was their fidelity to God's grace in a supreme moment of sacrifice. For most of us, it will be the day-by-day, year-to-year faithfulness to God's graces offering the prolonged martyrdom of our Christian vocation.

In all of this, we know that we have the loving intercession and help of a mother who earned her title, Queen of Martyrs.

43

Queen of Confessors
Queen of Virgins
Queen of Confessors
and Virgins

Queen of Confessors

When St. Martin of Tours died, there was general agreement that he was an exemplary Christian and a remarkably holy man. But up until that time, only those who had given up their lives in martyrdom were given the title "saint."

St. John the Evangelist, for instance, while he had not actually died under the sword, was so tortured, and so ready to pay the supreme sacrifice, that he was given the title of martyr and honored as a saint.

Of the first fifty popes, all but two are honored as saints, and most of those were martyrs. When the age of the martyrs ended and the Church continued to produce saintly men and women, how were they to be honored?

Never underestimate the ingenuity of Christian devotion. The martyrs, it was decided, had professed their faith with the shedding of their blood. The rest "confessed" their faith by the power of their holy lives.

So, St. Martin of Tours could indeed be honored as a saint, and the procession of saintly confessors began. The canonization process, simple as it might have been to start with, was under the direction of the local bishop.

Unfortunately, this produced such a plethora of saints that Rome was ultimately forced to step in and reserve this right to itself. Before that happened, however, every city and village, in Ireland, England, France and the rest of the Catholic areas, had its own list of local saints. The criteria were very, very loose. About all that was needed was for a person to die "in the odor of sanctity."

When Rome reserved the canonization process to itself, popes such as Urban VIII made some very strict rules. These have been relaxed some, but not a great deal.

Now these confessors come from almost every state in life, from almost every vocation. When we term Mary as Queen of Confessors we not only state that her confession of Christianity was the first and greatest, we also acknowledge that she is the Queen Mother of all who believe, of all the members of the Church.

A saint is canonized not because he performed extraordinary actions — walking on water as St. Raymond of Penyafort did, levitation as St. Joseph of Cupertino did, the stigmata of Christ as St. Francis of Assisi had — no, a saint is canonized because he or she was a heroic model of faith, hope and charity.

Being the recipient of important visions is not enough. It wasn't enough that Juan Diego received the *tilma* from Mary at Guadalupe. The visions at Lourdes are not mentioned once in the canonization papers of St. Bernardette Soubirous. The same is true for St. Catherine Laboure and the visions that resulted in the Miraculous Medal. The list could go on.

There has been some mild protest about the introduction of the cause of Father Junipero Serra. They claim that he was too strict with his converts, even unjust. They want to judge him in the light of a twentieth-century, civil-rights worker!

What they miss is not that Serra baptized thousands of pagans, or walked thousands of miles in his missionary work, or founded the first missions in the State of California. If he is ever canonized, it will be because he was heroic in his practice of faith, hope, and charity. His good works are important only insofar as they spring from these virtues. Faith comes alive by works of charity.

Mary is the Lady of these holy people, she is their Queen, because her life as a Christian inspired them. When you examine the lives of almost all the canonized saints, at least since the Reformation, you will find they all have a remarkable devotion to the Blessed Mother.

St. Charles Borromeo is the very ideal of a reformation-minded bishop, after the Council of Trent, the model of a Tridentine Counter-reformation pastoral prelate. In the original prayer for his Office, the Church proclaimed that "Pastoral solicitude rendered him glorious."

He convened synods to which he compelled the suffragan bishops in his province to attend. He was active in pastoral visitations and confirmations, and he founded the Oblates of St. Ambrose. He worked untiringly for the reform and renewal of the Church in his territory and became the model for other bishops in this work.

For all his decrees and directives and sermons, he always found time for devotion to the holy Mother of God, and constantly encouraged it in his diocese.

In the first chapter of his Rules for the Oblates of St. Ambrose, he placed the group under the special patronage of the "ever-virgin Mother of God." For their spiritual exercises he ordained that special Marian devotions be held every day.

He ordered that every church in the territory of Milan have "a painting, statue or sculpture of the Blessed Virgin Mary and of its own Patron Saint."

He encouraged frequent Holy Communion for all his people, and especially on the principle feast of the liturgical year "and on all the greater feasts of the Blessed Virgin Mary." Known for his reform of the seminary training system for priests, he ordered that the Little Office of the Blessed Mother be recited every day, as well as the Rosary, or Corona, as it was called then. He encouraged all in major orders to belong to a Marian Sodality.

The confessors come from every walk of life, from popes and kings and queens, to humble men like St. Benedict, Joseph Labre, and St. Martin de Porres. They include founders of the great religious Orders — Benedict, Bernard, Francis, Dominic, Ignatius, Vincent de Paul, Paul of the Cross, and Alphonsus Liguori.

The women are there, too, in great numbers and especially those who started the great religious Orders and Congregations. We have Scholastica, Ursula, Clare, Louise de Marillac, Jane Francis de Chantal, and growing hosts of others.

Even the widows are honored with special devotion. The only vocation not honored as such, are the married saints. Not one has yet been canonized with the simple title "mother" or "father," "husband" or "wife," with the notable exceptions of St. Joseph and some scriptural saints.

Could it be because the married vocation is the ordinary route to Heaven and the Church expects to see most of them there? However, for the needs of our day, to point up this sacred vocation, we may now need to institute that designation.

Whatever the case, Mary as the Queen of the Confessors has earned this title and it is an inspiration to all of us to join her clients in this profession of living faith. Because we honor Mary, our faith in Jesus is firmer and more fruitful.

Queen of Virgins
The perpetual virginity of the Mother of God is praised in the title "Holy Virgin of virgins," or in the newer translation, "Most Honored of virgins."

It is her glory, the triumph of God's power in her, that before, during, and after childbirth she remained ever a virgin. (This was treated in Chapter Four.)

The four great Marian Doctors of the Church, Anselm, Bernard, Bonaventure, and Peter Damian never ceased to praise this singular privilege, along with her complete and ever-sinless state.

"Immaculate" and "ever-virgin" are two of the praises that spring up most universally in the writings of the saints in the East and the West, in century after century.

It is firmly proclaimed in the *magisterium* of the Church by popes, bishops and theologians. Under this title, we praise Mary as the Queen of Virgins, of those called and most willing to imitate Jesus and Mary in this virginal vocation.

Note well that it is a counsel of perfection and that not all are called to it. Our Lord pointed out, "Not all can accept this, but only those to whom that is granted. Some are incapable of marriage because they were born so; some, because they were made so by others; some, because they renounced marriage for the sake of the kingdom of heaven. Whoever can accept this ought to accept it" (Mt 19:11-12).

The motivation for virginity and celibacy must be a supernatural one, the imitation of Jesus and Mary, with total dedication to God and neighbor as the result. To be virtuous it must be undertaken "for the sake of the kingdom of heaven."

St. Paul writes about this: "I should like you to be free of anxiety. An unmarried man is anxious about the things of the Lord, how he may please the Lord. But a married man is anxious about the things of the world, how he may please his wife, and he is divided.

"An unmarried woman or a virgin is anxious about the things of the Lord, so that she may be holy both in body and spirit. A married woman, on the other hand, is anxious about the things of the world, how she may please her husband. I am telling you this for your own benefit, not to impose a restraint on you, but for the sake of propriety and adherence to the Lord without distraction" (1 Cor 7:32-35).

The married vocation, so sacred in Christ, so holy as a path to Heaven, so powerful as a sacrament, has its own rules for growth. This includes both the husband-wife relationship and the parent-child relationship. The use of the sexual powers and human sexuality in marriage are both holy as an exercise of love and a reflection of the union of Christ and the Church.

Dorothy Day in many of her columns called "On Pilgrimage" in the *Catholic Worker* weighs the beauty of the image of God in sex. The Christian Family Movement (CFM) has made great strides in promoting the matrimonial vocation as a Christian way of perfection.

But the fact does remain, as St. Paul points out, that marriage demands great sacrifices and a great outpouring of human love between husband and wife and in attentive, sensitive family relationships. Indeed, it is a way of perfection!

But the virgin and the celibate have the time and the opportunity to place the same sensitive love and sacrifice directly to the service of God and neighbor. Through the vows of religion, these people are freed to live a life of evangelical virtue without worrying about the rights of a partner who may well have other needs.

It is the glory of the Church throughout its history that countless numbers of men and women have taken up the direct service of God in this way. From the early desert fathers to the modern religious congregations and secular institutions, from dedicated, vowed missionaries to their lay helpers, the workers have gone out into the harvest to work for Christ and His Church directly.

We must ask this most holy and Immaculate of Virgins to pray to the Lord of the harvest to continue to send workers into the world.

St. John had a special vision of virgins in his Book of Revelation: "Then I looked and saw where the Lamb stood on Mount Zion, in the midst of a company of one hundred and forty-four thousand, with his Name and his Father's Name written on their foreheads. And I heard a sound from heaven, louder than water in full flood, or heavy thunder. The sound which I heard seemed to come from harpers playing their harps.

"They sang a new song there before the throne and the living figures and the elders. It was a song none else might learn to sing except the one hundred and forty-four thousand that came ransomed from the earth.

"These have kept their virginity untouched by a woman; these are the Lamb's attendants, wherever he goes. These have been ransomed for God and the Lamb as the first-fruits of mankind. Falsehood was not found on their lips; they stand there untainted before the throne of God" (Rv 14:1-5).

The Church has always valued virginity and celibacy as a special charisma that dedicates men and women to God. It is also a very special witness to the beauty of marriage. If the use of sexuality in marriage is a God-given gift and a praiseworthy tribute to God, then abstinence from its use as a sacrifice of love is a very acceptable gift to God. We would not want to give God anything less perfect. If human sexuality were not a "good," abstinence from it would not be something better or more perfect.

Some modern writers are urging changes in the Church's regard for celibacy. This is not the place to weigh the reasons, but we can hope that the Church will do nothing to lessen its glorious witness and its valuable tribute to God. Changes may be inevitable, but they should be made cautiously.

Mary, as Queen of Virgins, has a very special love for the fact and the virtue of virginity and celibacy, and for those who are thus dedicated.

44

Queen of All Saints

"After this I had a vision of a great multitude, which no one could count, from every nation, race, people, and tongue. They stood before the throne, and before the Lamb, wearing white robes and holding palm branches in their hands. . . . These are the ones who have survived the time of great distress; they have washed their robes and made them white in the blood of the Lamb. . . . And God will wipe away every tear from their eyes" (Rv 7:9,14,17).

This great multitude which no one can number is the host of saints who will enter Heaven until the end of time. A precious few will be canonized saints, but the vast majority will be those who have lived up to the graces God has given them and faithfully and loyally worked out their salvation.

Chief among the saints will be Mary, the Queen of Saints. As we have seen throughout this book, Mary's sanctity so far outdistances all the other saints combined that we are at a loss for words to describe it. God has adorned her soul with such great gifts that all the angels and saints rejoice to proclaim her their Queen.

In every seminary throughout the world, All Saints Day is a very special feast. It is always pointed out that we hope that this will some day be our own feast day.

The choirs prepared great music, the sacristans brought out the best vestments and sanctuary ornaments, and the cook provided a great dinner. The liturgical Office itself was a wonder of detail. Praising God for what His grace can do in mere mortals, we praise Mary, St. Joseph, the Apostles, and down through the ranks, until we come "to the vast multitude unable to be numbered."

Since Mary is Queen of All Saints, it is a good idea

to look a little more closely at the notion of sanctity in the Church. We can turn to that master of spiritual directors, Abbot Columba Marmion, O.S.B. Born in Dublin in 1858 of Irish and French parents, he was ordained in Rome in 1881 and five years later asked to be admitted to the Benedictine Abbey of Maredsous in Belgium, where eventually he would serve as abbot for more than a dozen years, until his death on January 30, 1923.

He was famous for his spiritual conferences which were published in three volumes, *Christ the Life of the Soul, Christ in His Mysteries* and *Christ the Ideal of the Monk*. He died before he could complete *Christ the Ideal of the Priest*, but he left enough that, with his notes, it was published posthumously. I edited an anthology of his work on the Holy Spirit, titled *Fire of Love*.

In *Christ in His Mysteries*, his concluding conference is for the Feast of All Saints, titled, "Christ the Crown of All the Saints." In the introduction to the conference, he outlines his ideas, especially about the notion of sanctification, that is, union with Christ.

" 'The God and Father of Our Lord Jesus Christ . . . has subjected all things under his feet, and has made him Head over all the Church which is his Body, and the fullness of him who is filled all in all' (Eph 1:3,22-23). These words of St. Paul show us the mystery of Christ Jesus considered in His Mystical Body, which is the Church.

"In all the preceding conferences we have had the joy of contemplating the Person of Jesus himself, his states, his abasements, his conflicts, his greatness, his triumph; we have not been able to turn our gaze away from his adorable Humanity which is for us the example of every virtue and the one source of every grace.

"But all the mysteries of the God-Man tend to the establishment and sanctification of the Church: 'for us and for our salvation' (Credo). Christ came in order to form to himself a society which might appear glorious before him 'not having spot or wrinkle or any such thing; but holy and without blemish' (Eph 5:27).

"So close and intimate is the union contracted with the Church that he is the Vine and she forms the branches; that he is the Head and she forms the body; that he is the Bridegroom and she has the rank of Bride. United together they compose what St. Augustine, in *The Unity of the Church*, so well calls the 'Whole Christ.'

"Christ and the Church are inseparable; one is not to be conceived of without the other. . . . We must speak of the Church that St. Paul calls the 'completing' of Christ and without which the mystery of Christ does not attain its perfection."

St. Cyprian, also writing on *The Unity of the Church*, comments along these same lines: "He cannot have God as a Father who does not have the Church as a mother. . . . He cannot possess the garment of Christ who tears and divides the Church of Christ."

Since the Mystical Body of Christ is the Church, that is, Christ and His members, that Body in Heaven comes to its perfection in the eternal union of Christ and the saints.

What we proclaim in the title Mary, Queen of All Saints, is a further acknowledgement of Mary's position in the Church. Because God wills it, Mary is the crowning glory of this whole heavenly Kingdom.

Christ wills that all the graces He bestows on mankind must come through the hands of Mary. She is the channel He uses. "In this way," says Pope John Paul II, "Mary's motherhood continues unceasingly in the Church as the mediation which intercedes, and the Church expresses her faith in this truth by invoking Mary under the titles of Advocate, Auxiliatrix, Adjutrix and Mediatrix." He takes these titles from the Second Vatican Council, *Lumen Gentium* (No. 62).

The lives of the saints contain so many examples of

this maternal care that Mary has for her clients. One of the most notable is St. Therese of Lisieux. As a young child, she was at the brink of death and she prayed and begged the Blessed Mother to have pity on her. The statue of Our Lady in the girl's bedroom smiled at her, and she came back to health.

When her family went to Rome in 1887, there was one particular devotion Therese wanted to perform. She went to the shrine of Our Lady of Victory to pray that she would be allowed to enter Carmel although she was so young, and to help her become a saint. How magnificently that prayer was answered!

St. Gertrude expresses the essence of Mariology in her well-known prayer. But then the saints knew their Queen Mother so well!

"O fairest lily, lovable Mary, you are, after God, my greatest, surest hope, speak for me in the presence of your dear Son, speak for me one effectual word.

"Plead my cause with all your loving devotedness; in your goodness obtain for me the object and aim of my desires; for I trust in you who are, after Jesus, my one and only hope.

"Show yourself a tender mother to me; obtain for me that I be received by Our Lord into the secret place of his love, into that school where the Holy Spirit teaches. You above all others can obtain this favor from your divine Son.

"O Mother most faithful, surround your daughter with your thoughtful care that I may become an ever-living treasure of love, that I may grow in holiness, and that the dew from Heaven may uphold me in perseverance."

45

Queen Conceived Without Original Sin

Bishop Charles Francis Buddy was the first bishop of San Diego, California (1936-1966). For many years he sponsored a "Crusade for Souls" and actually taught adult convert classes himself. Among his books is *For Them Also*, which grew out of these classes and contains a look at the fundamentals of Catholicism.

Whenever he had to speak about the Blessed Mother, he was at his best and most eloquent. Among his favorite feasts were the Immaculate Conception and the Assumption.

"The victory of Our Savior," he notes, "includes the victory of the woman, His Mother, over the enemy of mankind. Moreover, it was the eternal plan of God the Father to prepare a dignified and spotless dwelling place for His divine Son.

"St. John the Baptizer was sanctified in his mother's womb. The Blessed Virgin Mary merited an even higher degree of divine grace, in proportion to her dignity, by being preserved from original sin.

"When Pope Pius IX defined the doctrine of the Immaculate Conception on December 8, 1854, he did not create a new doctrine, because the Immaculate Conception of the Blessed Virgin Mary had always been true and had been believed by the faithful for many centuries.

"The Pope simply confirmed the doctrine that had already existed and took it out of the realm of doubt or controversy."

For on that morning of December 8, 1854, the Vatican Court, with all the pomp and circumstances it could muster, assembled to hear Pope Pius IX read the

Bull *Ineffabilis Deus*, and formally define and promulgate, conscious that he was the successor to Saints Peter and Paul, to the whole world:

Mary, "in the first instance of her conception, by a singular privilege and grace, granted by God in view of the merits of Jesus Christ, the Saviour of the human race, was preserved exempt from original sin" (Denz. 1641).

Original Sin means that the human race, and each individual, enters the world lacking the grace or direct friendship of God. The book of Genesis presents this in the sin of Adam and Eve (chapter 3). The exact nature of that sin will be debated by Bible scholars, no doubt, until the end of time. The fact remains that the gift of original justice that adorned the souls of the first man and woman were lost.

How that wound is repaired consists of the whole economy of salvation. The Redeemer promised, the prophecies fulfilled, and the infinite sacrifice of Jesus Christ on Calvary comprise the one drama of our salvation. Every member of the human race needs the justification won by Christ, and bestowed in such total freedom through the grace of faith and baptism.

Did Mary need the grace of Christ to be redeemed? Absolutely!

And that absolute need was the cause for most of the controversy around the doctrine of Mary's Immaculate Conception. The unanimous witness of the Fathers and Doctors of the Church to Mary's perpetual sinlessness had to be reconciled with this total dependence on the merits of Christ for salvation.

But, if this doctrine in any way impugned the need for everyone to be saved by Christ's action, then there was a fatal flaw in it. Saints as great as Augustine and Thomas Aquinas had trouble with it at this point, even though they were aware of the ancient teaching about Mary's sinlessness.

Duns Scotus is usually credited with the answer

that solved the dilemma. We are saved because the grace of Christ is freely given after we are created. In Mary's case, God anticipated the grace of Christ and preserved Mary from all stain of sin, even Original Sin, by applying that grace at the instant of her conception.

Note that physically, humanly speaking, the biology of Mary's birth was like all human beings. Through the interaction of her parents, traditionally named St. Joachim and St. Ann, she was conceived. Through the intervention of Almighty God, she was preserved from sin by the anticipated application of the grace of Christ.

Some would confuse this with the Virgin Birth, but any Catholic schoolchild knows that that refers to Our Lord's Nativity, that He was born of the Virgin Mary without human male seed. That He was "immaculately" conceived goes without saying, since the Person there is the Son of God, the Second Person of the Most Holy Trinity.

Mary's Immaculate Conception was a tremendous and indeed, singular, privilege.

Now, once this is established, what other effects go along with it? Death, hardship, travail and all sorts of sorrows came into the world with Original Sin (Gn 3:14-19). All we have to do, in fact, is look around and survey the human condition.

But since Mary is preserved from this, did she escape the effects of Original Sin. The general consensus of the writers is that she did. Her mind was not clouded nor her will weakened. She could go immediately to the truths she sought, and her love of God and neighbor had no limits, beyond her physical capacity.

Some, like St. Alphonsus, give her complete infused knowledge from the instant of her conception and have her act on it immediately. I wonder if this is literally true, much as I would like to agree.

Her Son, while being the Son of God also, had to go back to Nazareth, at the age of twelve, "and advance in wisdom and age and favor before God and man" (Lk

2:52). His human nature, the instrument of His Divinity in the work of salvation, had to go through the stages of normal maturing. For instance, I strongly doubt that at His nativity He knew physically how to use the tools of Joseph's trade. This was part of the wisdom and knowledge in which He grew.

So with Mary, her body was the instrument of that soul, with all its privileges and infused knowledge. But it is hard to understand how at the age of three, for instance, at her Presentation in the Temple, she could make the tremendous spiritual offerings that some relate. She, too, had to grow physically, and as her body and mind became more mature, her spiritual life would grow.

St. Luke seems to indicate this when he concludes his account of the Child Jesus among the teachers in the Temple. "But they did not understand what he said to them. . . . And his mother kept all these things in her heart" (Lk 2:50-51).

That may be interesting as a speculation, but the fact remains that Mary's Immaculate Conception has special meaning for us in the United States. In 1846, years before it was a defined doctrine, the bishops in the United States had proclaimed Mary under the title of her Immaculate Conception as the patroness of the country.

All over the New World, North and South America, the missionaries who brought the good news of Christ to the native Americans brought with them an especial love of Mary. It's not a coincidence that one of the largest and most important cities in the United States is dedicated to Our Lady of the Angels, Los Angeles.

Even before Our Lady appeared at Guadalupe, within a generation of the arrival of Columbus, there were place names and mission settlements dedicated to Mary. Since then, wherever Catholic missionaries appeared, the geographic locations named after Mary's various titles become almost too numerous to list.

We ask Mary Immaculate to bless us in the service of her Son. How easily the prayer comes to our lips, "O Mary, conceived without sin, pray for us who have recourse to you." What confidence we have in her powerful intercession with a Son so powerful that He could preserve her from all sin!

Bishop Buddy always closed his class on the *Immaculata* with the lines that are so familiar from the non-Catholic poet William Wordsworth:

Mother, whose virgin bosom was uncrossed
By the least shade of thought to sin allied,
Woman! Above all women glorified—
Our tainted nature's solitary boast.

46

Queen Assumed Into Heaven

By the Apostolic Constitution *Munificentissimus Deus*, Pope Pius XII, on November 1, 1950, defined the Assumption of Our Lady as a dogma of faith. The essential passage is, "We pronounce, declare and define it to be a divinely revealed dogma: that the Immaculate Mother of God, the ever Virgin Mary having completed the course of her earthly life, was assumed body and soul to heavenly glory."

This is the culmination of many centuries of commonly accepted facts believed about the Mother of God. Feasts in honor of Our Lady's Assumption, or Dormition (Falling Asleep) go back to the sixth century, attesting to a belief that was even older.

No city, no matter how ancient or holy, has ever claimed to have the relics of the Blessed Mother. Both Ephesus and Jerusalem claim to have her tomb, but neither has ever claimed her body. Tradition seems to favor Jerusalem.

Several questions emerge from the papal definition. There is no direct scriptural basis for the doctrine, but those that validate Mary's claim to divine maternity certainly include all her other prerogatives. Pope Pius XII was satisfied with that.

The question the pope asked the bishops of the Catholic world was twofold. Is the Assumption definable, i.e. is it a matter of divine faith? Second, is it opportune at this time to proclaim publicly what is accepted privately?

The cardinals, bishops and experts whom the pope consulted were nearly unanimous in stating their belief in the Assumption as a part of the divine treasury of the Faith. I say "nearly unanimous" since the few that did not feel it was definable were so minor as to be negligible. Only a few more felt that it was not an opportune time to define it.

So, Pope Pius XII showed his own deep faith in and devotion to the Mother of God by this solemn definition. It is indeed a satisfying doctrine because it completes so beautifully the holy cycle of Mary's earthly life.

From her Immaculate Conception in the womb of her mother, St. Ann, to the end of her life when she joined her Son, in triumph through her Assumption, we have a full life thoroughly embraced within the circle of her Son's love and example.

Did the Blessed Mother die, or was her passing to eternal life through a "falling asleep" process, until she went body and soul into heaven? Pope Pius did not settle that question, nor could he on the available historical evidence that we have.

As a matter of devout speculation, there are those who say that her immaculate body was exempted from the penalty for Adam's sin. As the New Eve, she did not fall under that category of death. Certainly, it was not necessary that she die.

That she did die is the conclusion of most of the writers who consider the question. It is equally as certain that Christ did not have to die as a penalty for His sins. He was sinless. He chose to die as the acceptable sacrifice in our stead. In that sense, that He was fulfilling the Scriptures, He could tell the disciples on the way to Emmaus that the Messiah had to die.

Because Mary's life is the first and best Christian following of Christ, her imitation of His activities are of the highest order. Because He actually did die, so did she.

St. John Damascene has some very enlightening thoughts on the subject. Speaking of the "Dormition of the Blessed Virgin," he says, "Today the Immaculate Virgin in whom there is no spot of human taint, but only the love of heavenly delights, today she returns not to dust but she is brought into the mansions of

Heaven — she, herself, a living Heaven! From her the source of all life was given to mankind. How then could she ever taste death?

"She yielded to that law decreed by Him whom she had borne. As a daughter of Adam she submitted to that ancient law, for her Son, who is life itself, had not refused it. However, as the Mother of the Living God she was rightfully brought up to him. . . .

"Where I am, says the Life and the Truth, there shall my servant be. How much more so, then, that his Mother should be joined to him."

"That Mary is Queen," states St. Bonaventure, "and outstanding in her glory is chanted by the psalmist in that psalm (45:10) especially prophetical of Christ and his Mother. First he says of Christ, 'Your throne, O God, exists forever,' Then he adds of Our Lady, 'The Queen shall sit at your right side.' This indicates her outstanding power.

"He follows this with the words, 'Robed in gold' to express the glorious gift of corporal immortality shown by her Assumption. Never could it happen that the body which enveloped the Word-made-flesh, which was perfectly sanctified on earth, could ever return to dust, to be the food of worms."

St. Peter Canisius also pays tribute to Mary on the Feast of the Assumption. "Emmanuel entered this world as a stranger, but you received him into your world as into a palatial manor. Today you are received by him into the regal palace of Heaven, to have him bestow on you the place of honor worthy of the Mother of such a Solomon.

"Happy the day on which so precious a treasure is transferred from the desert of this world to the joy of the eternal city. All the blessed of Heaven rejoice on this exceedingly joyful day.

"Happy the day on which the gentle, loving Bride finds that which her souls seeks, receives that which she has prayed for, takes possession finally of all that she has hoped for — the eternal vision of God."

"Certainly the highest angels," writes Francis Suarez, "welcomed Christ on the Day of his Ascension, as they probably did on the Day of his Resurrection as well.

"We can believe the same about the Blessed Virgin on the Day of her Assumption. If it is true (as is piously believed and as the Fathers themselves thought) that Christ himself came down and assisted in the heavenly ascent of his Mother, certainly the angels did, too."

"Death being the punishment of sin," states St. Alphonsus Liguori, "it would seem that the divine Mother — all holy and exempt as she was from its slightest stain — should also have been exempt from death, and from encountering the misfortunes to which the children of Adam, infected by the poison of sin, are subject.

"But God was pleased that Mary should in all things resemble Jesus; and as the Son died, it was becoming that the Mother should also die; because, moreover he wished to give to the just the example of the precious death prepared for them, he willed that even the most Blessed Virgin should die, but by a sweet and happy death."

When Pope Pius XII ordered that this title be added to the Litany of Loreto, he gave us all the opportunity to exercise our Christian imagination in trying to picture the joyful reception of Mary into Heaven. God's grace has triumphed completely in Mary, and all of Heaven rejoices.

And, it is our pious hope, of course, that Jesus and Mary will someday welcome us into Heaven, first our souls, and at the end of time, our bodies. Therefore, the vistas suggested by this Marian title are almost limitless.

47

Queen of the Most Holy Rosary
Queen of the Rosary

Americans are noted for being practical people. We like things that work, that fulfill what they promise, that "measure up." Saints and scholars, popes and theologians have joined in praising and recommending the Rosary of Our Lady for five centuries, but it appeals to us Americans because it works.

From contemplatives in their monasteries to truck drivers rolling down the highways, the Rosary is the most popular private prayer known to us. It has a power and a mystique all of its own to bind us to Jesus through Mary, through joys and sorrows and triumphs — theirs and ours.

The Rosary devotion as we know it was introduced by Blessed Alan de la Roche, a Dominican who lived in the fifty middle years of the fifteenth century. He piously referred it to his founder, St. Dominic, and while it is true to the spirit of Dominic and has roots in other, older Marian forms, Blessed Alan deserves the credit.

In 1479, four years after Alan's death, Pope Sixtus IV became the first of a long line of popes who gave the Rosary their special commendation. But the laity themselves took to the Rosary as to a natural devotion.

In fact, it soon earned the name "The Psalter of the Poor," or "The Poor Man's Breviary." The monks and nuns gathered together in their chapels to chant or recite the Divine Office, which, at heart, has the 150 Psalms to center its liturgical piety.

Since most of the people did not know how to read,

nor did they consider this a great deprivation I must add, when they gathered for the Hours of the Breviary, they would silently recite prayers that they had memorized.

The 150 *Aves* of the Rosary imitated the 150 Psalms, and the divisions by tens into decades makes counting them on the fingers quite easy and effortless. Beads to reflect this division were a logical consequence of the devotion. After all, if you want to say ten prayers or 150, you like to know how far you are, and when you are finished. This is not unique to Christianity.

But the great power of the Rosary comes from the fifteen meditations or mysteries. Through the five Joyful Mysteries, the Infancy Narratives of St. Matthew and St. Luke really come alive. They glow with incarnational theology and because of them, many a devout lay person has a keener grasp of the Incarnation than some learned theologians or Bible scholars.

The Sorrowful Mysteries do the same thing for the theology of Redemption. The saving Passion and death of Christ take on an even deeper meaning by this prayerful interaction with His actions. The evil of mortal sin becomes strikingly evident from the price that was paid, the sacrifice that was made, to atone for them.

Finally the Glorious Mysteries make the eschatological dimensions of the Paschal events a vivid motivation for the person praying. That Jesus and Mary reign triumphantly in Heaven is the first step, because we are called to go to them. Jesus Christ is the firstborn from the dead (Col 1:18). Then, the work of the Holy Spirit, guaranteeing the Church in truth and giving it life until the end of time, makes Pentecost a present reality for us.

The clients of Our Lady of the Rosary find great joy and comfort in its history. Among the great events associated with this devotion is the great naval victory of the Christians over the Moslems at Lepanto on October

7, 1571. Pope St. Pius V urged Christians to fast and pray to save Christendom from the hands of the infidels. Their record of pillaging and enslaving Christians was notorious. The prayer that this saintly pontiff, who was a Dominican, decreed was the Rosary.

After the victory was announced, he proclaimed that day the Feast of Our Lady of the Rosary and he said, "By the Rosary the darkness of heresy has been dispelled and the light of the Catholic Faith shines out in all its brilliancy."

During the centuries when the English rule in Ireland became so brutal, when the Faith was proscribed and the persecution was so violent, the Irish went off into the passes and byways to pray their Rosaries alone and in groups.

When they escaped to the New World or went in brutal penal ships to Australia, it was the Rosary that sustained their Faith. The menial jobs they took in America, where they lived not much better than the slaves, were made tolerable by the Rosary. It sustained them until they could better themselves.

During the years of the French Revolution and during the trying times that came after, the peasants of France and central Europe clung to their Rosaries. When Our Lady appeared to Bernardette at Lourdes, the youngster fell to her knees and started her Rosary. And the Blessed Mother approved and took up the Rosary beads that hung at her side.

At Fatima, the Blessed Mother again approved the Rosary, as she has at most private revelations in recent centuries. While the emphasis of Our Lady at Guadalupe was the rights of the native, modern pilgrims all pray their Rosaries when they are there.

Pope Leo XIII was the great modern devotee of the Rosary and it was he who designated October as the Month of the Rosary. He published many works on the Rosary and never ceased to urge it on others.

"To appease the might of an outraged God," he

states in *Octobri Mense,* "and to bring the health of soul so needed by those who are sorely afflicted, there is nothing better than devout prayer and persevering prayer, provided that it be joined with a love and practice of Christian life. And both of these, the spirit of prayer and the practice of Christian life, are best attained through the devotion of the Rosary of Mary. . . .

"To this commendation of the Rosary which follows from the very nature of the prayer, we may add that the Rosary offers an easy way to present the chief mysteries of the Christian religion and to impress them upon the mind; and this commendation is one of the most beautiful of all.

"For it is mainly by faith that one sets out on the straight and sure path to God and learns to revere in mind and heart his supreme majesty, his sovereignty over the whole creation, his undoubted power, wisdom and providence."

Pope Pius XI adds, "Among the various supplications with which we successfully appeal to the Virgin Mother of God, the Holy Rosary without doubt occupies a special and distinct place."

And Pope Paul VI, following the lead of Vatican Council II writes of the Rosary, "This prayer is well-suited to the People of God, most pleasing to the Mother of God and most effective in gaining heaven's blessings."

Some have worried about the repetitious usage of the Rosary prayers. St. Teresa of Avila offers this advice. "Before we being reciting the Hours, or the Rosary, we should consider whom we are going to address, and who we are that are addressing him, so that we may do so in the way we should.

"I assure you that if you give all due attention to a consideration of these two points before beginning vocal prayers which you are about to say, you would be engaging in mental prayer for a very long time."

And the retired Archbishop of St. Louis, John Cardinal Carberry, reminds us, "The Rosary is strength, it is power, it is a chain of gold which links us to Mary."

In the book *My Rosary: Its Power and Mystery* (Alba House) I have also suggested some alternatives to the standard fifteen Mysteries, especially for private devotions. It is very useful and adds a little variety, to meditate on some of the other Gospel passages, such as the beatitudes, the marriage feast at Cana, the election of the Apostles etc. It gives great scope to the Christian imagination.

Various prayers have been suggested to conclude the Rosary. One of the most beautiful is, "O God, whose only begotten Son by his Life, Death and Resurrection has purchased for us the rewards of eternal life, grant we beseech you, that meditating upon these mysteries in the Most Holy Rosary of the Blessed Virgin Mary, we may both imitate what they contain and obtain what they promise: through the same Christ, Our Lord. Amen."

48

Queen of Peace

Death is the immediate fruit of Original Sin and, all the disorders that afflict human nature come from that source. But wars, tortures, and the various brutalities that man inflicts upon man must have, as their immediate cause, actual sin. Whoever coined the phrase "Man's inhumanity to man" really described one of the effects of mortal sin and its fruits.

This Marian title Queen of Peace is an ancient plea on the part of the Church for her intercession to bring peace to mankind. Peace is not just the absence of war, but it is the possession of all that we need to fulfill our true human dignity.

In the nineteenth century, popular devotion exalted Mary's title "Help of Christians," but when World War I enveloped Europe, Pope Benedict XV added the title "Queen of Peace" to the Litany to beg for this grace, peace in the world.

The idealists on this side of the Atlantic, led by President Wilson, spoke of "the war to end all wars," and they conceived the League of Nations as an insurmountable barrier to future wars. But the politicians of Europe were sowing the seeds of World War II even as they talked of peace.

The Versailles Treaty which ended World War I was the first major European treaty which did not have papal representation. Neither did the one which ended World War II and the seeds of the Cold War and the United Nations brought on the same uneasy "peace." Some claim it is more like a truce than real peace.

Pope Pius XI ordered that this title of Our Lady should be a permanent addition to the Litany. It is a necessary reminder that there will be no lasting peace without God. The frightful advances in nuclear warfare have made a laughing stock out of the "just war" theory, since a nuclear war will probably cause most life on earth to cease. "Nuclear deterrence" is a frightening alternative.

It would seem that we must redouble our efforts to gain Mary's intercession for world peace and justice. Our prayers are not just for the absence of war between East and West, but for the removal of the causes of injustice which promote war.

Idealists now are talking of "Spaceship Earth" and "The Global Village." But if they divorce these concepts from God, then the peace of Christ will not reign over the earth. Realists will remind us that as long as man has free will, the reality of sin and its disasters will remain.

This must not dissuade us from making an all-out effort for peace in the world, and peace of mind, heart and soul in all individuals. It's more than idealistic; it is utopian. But, if we can't achieve Heaven on earth, then we must strive for whatever part of it that is humanly possible.

Christ is the Prince of Peace, as Isaiah prophesied: "A Child is born to us and his name shall be called — the Prince of Peace" (Is 9:6). And in his spiritual kingdom, "The wolf shall dwell with the lamb; and the leopard shall lie down with the kid; the calf and the lion and the sheep will abide together, and a little Child shall lead them" (Is 11:6).

When Christ was born at Bethlehem, the angels exulted, "Glory to God in the highest and peace on earth to men of good will" (Lk 2:14). There was the *Pax Romana* imposed on the then known world when Jesus was born, but it was just that — an imposition. Justice and living conditions under the Romans were far from ideal. The Holy Family lived as peasants, "people of the land," with whom Mary identified in her *Magnificat*.

The peace bestowed by Christ is a spiritual gift and it presupposes good will. The only lasting exterior peace comes from the interior peace of people of good intentions and efforts. Christ offers us peace of soul as the beginning of all works of peace. Mary, the peaceful Mother of Nazareth, learned this from her intimate association with Jesus.

When Christ went forth to His Public Life, He established the charter of His Kingdom and with the beatitudes. Chief among them was peace: "Blessed are the peacemakers, for they shall be called the children of God" (Mt 5:9). Among His last words before His Passion and death were "Peace I leave with you. My peace I give you" (Jn 14:27).

After the Resurrection His constant greeting was "Peace!" When He gave His Church the Sacrament of Reconciliation, the power to forgive sins, it was with the blessing of peace. Peace must be founded on friendship with God; the reconciliation of sinful man with God is the only foundation for peace.

St. Basil the Great comments on this notion of peace: "Concerning this peace the Lord has said, 'peace I leave with you, my peace do I give you.' Seek, therefore, after the peace of the Lord and pursue it. And you will not pursue it otherwise than by running toward the goal, to the prize of the heavenly calling. For true peace is from above.

"Yet, as long as we are bound to the flesh, we are yoked to many things which also trouble us. Seek, then, after a peace, a release from the troubles of this world; possess a calm mind, a tranquil and unconfused state of soul which is neither agitated by the passions nor drawn aside by false doctrines that challenge by their persuasiveness to assent, in order that you may obtain 'the peace of God which surpasses all understanding and guards your heart.'

"He who seeks after peace seeks Christ because 'He Himself is our Peace,' who has made us into the new man, 'making peace through the blood of His Cross, whether on earth or in the heavens.'"

Mary, because of her Immaculate Conception, enjoyed that perfect peace of soul. She always enjoyed God's friendship. Her perfect imitation of Christ throughout her life made that all the more perfect. To call her the "Queen of Peace" is a logical conclusion to her way of life.

To ask her to let us share this gift with her is equally logical to Christian devotion. It means putting first things first. Friendship with God must come first, then the fruits of that interior peace may start to take effect beyond the individual.

In a world that seems to be determined to ruin itself, victory for the peace of Christ seems the proper note with which to end this little work. To urge this plea on Mary the Queen of Peace, is the best way to convey our urgency to the Sacred Heart of Jesus.

As St. Bernard reminds us, "With her protection, there is nothing to fear. Under her leadership you will succeed. With her encouragement, all is possible.

"And someday, you, yourself, will experience the depth of the meaning in St. Luke's phrase, 'And the Virgin's name was Mary!' With only these few phrases of meditation, we are strengthened in the clarity of her brilliance. How much greater strength we can derive from silent contemplation! In the scintillating light of this Star our fervent service of her Son will glow every more brilliant."

Alternate Litany

Litany of Mary of Nazareth

Courtesy of: Pax Christi USA, 348 E. 10th St., Erie, Pennsylvania *(for private use)*

Glory to you, God our Creator . . . Breathe into us new life, new meaning.
Glory to you, God our Savior . . . Lead us in the way of peace and justice.
Glory to you, healing Spirit . . . Transform us to impower others.

Mary, wellspring of peace . . . Be our guide.
Model of strength. . .
Model of gentleness. . .
Model of trust. . .
Model of courage. . .
Model of patience. . .
Model of risk. . .
Model of openness. . .
Model of perseverance. . .

Mother of the Liberator . . . pray for us.
Mother of the homeless. . .
Mother of the dying. . .
Mother of the non-violent. . .
Widowed Mother. . .
Mother of a political prisoner. . .
Mother of the condemned. . .
Mother of the executed criminal. . .

Oppressed woman . . . Lead us to life.
Liberator of the oppressed. . .
Marginalized woman. . .
Comforter of the afflicted. . .
Cause of our joy. . .

Sign of contradiction. . .
Breaker of bondage. . .
Political refugee. . .
Seeker of sanctuary. . .
First disciple. . .
Sharer in Christ's ministry. . .
Participant in Christ's Passion. . .
Seeker of God's will. . .
Witness to Christ's Resurrection. . .

Woman of mercy . . . Empower us!
Woman of faith. . .
Woman of contemplation. . .
Woman of vision. . .
Woman of wisdom and understanding. . .
Woman of grace and truth. . .
Woman, pregnant with hope. . .
Woman, centered in God. . .

Pray for us, O Holy Mother of God;
That we may be worthy of the promises of Christ.

Let us pray—
Mary, Queen of peace / we entrust our lives to you. /
Shelter us from war, hatred / and oppression.

Teach us / to live in peace, / to educate ourselves /
for peace.

Inspire us to act justly, / to revere all God has made,
/ to respect the gift of life, / to promote human dignity. /
Root peace firmly in our hearts / in our souls, / in our
neighbors, / and in the world.
Amen.

Index of Biblical Quotations

Index of Names